ADVANTAGE Grammar

Table of Contents

Table of Contents

CREDITS

Concept Development: Kent Publishing Services, Inc.

Written by: Martha Morss

Editor: Thomas Hatch

Design/Production: Signature Design Group, Inc.

Art Director: Tom Cochrane

Project Director: Carolea Williams

Introduction

The **Advantage Grammar** series for grades 3–8 offers instruction and practice in key writing skills, including
- grammar and usage
- capitalization and punctuation
- spelling
- writing good sentences
- writing good paragraphs
- editing your work

Take a look at all the advantages this grammar series offers . . .

Strong Skill Instruction
- The teaching component at the top of each lesson provides the support students need to work through the book independently.

- Plenty of skill practice pages will ensure students master essential skills they need to become competent writers.

- Examples, models, and practice activities use content from across the curriculum so students are learning about social studies, science, and literature as they master writing skills.

Editing Your Work pages provide for mixed practice of skills in a format that supports today's process approach to teaching writing.

Take a Test Drive pages provide practice using a test-taking format such as those included in national standardized and proficiency tests.

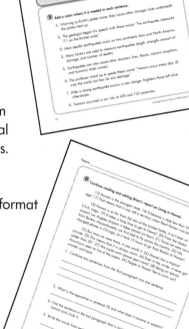

Name _____

Reviewing Nouns and Pronouns

1

ANCIENT CIVILIZATIONS OF ASIA

⭐ **Nouns and pronouns** have the same function: they name things.

A noun is a word that names a person, place, thing, or idea. A common noun is not specific and is lowercased. A proper noun is specific and is uppercased.

Person:	emperor, Genghis Khan	Thing:	palace, Taj Mahal
Place:	continent, Asia	Idea:	religion, Buddhism

A pronoun is a word that is used in place of a noun.

The girl gave Genghis Khan the message and then stared at **him**.

(*Him* is used in place of *Genghis Khan.*)

In sentences, nouns and pronouns are used as subjects and objects.

The **girl** *(subject)* gave **Genghis Khan** *(indirect object)* the **message** *(direct object)*.

She *(subject)* handed **it** *(direct object)* to the **emperor** *(object of preposition)*.

A **Underline the nouns in each sentence. Circle any pronouns you find.**

1. Genghis Khan was a ruler of the Mongols in the early 1200s.

2. The Mongols lived in central Asia on treeless plains called steppes.

3. They lived in clans related by kinship.

4. Several clans made up a tribe.

5. The chief of a tribe was elected based on courage, military ability, and leadership.

6. If a chief was greatly admired, men from other tribes would swear loyalty to him.

7. The Mongols developed amazing skill on horseback.

8. Because they could hold on to a horse with just their feet, they could shoot their weapons while they were riding.

9. Riding skill gave the soldiers a strong advantage in battle.

10. The great Khan and his warriors conquered a huge amount of land between Beijing and the Caspian Sea.

   Advantage Grammar Grade 7 © 2005 Creative Teaching Press

B Next to each noun, write *person, place, thing,* or *idea* to show what it refers to. If it is a proper noun, write the word *proper.*

1. warrior _____   6. feet _____

2. land _____   7. loyalty _____

3. courage _____   8. Khan _____

4. Asia _____   9. Beijing _____

5. advantage _____   10. Mongols _____

C Complete the chart by filling in an appropriate noun, proper noun, or pronoun.

	Common Noun	Proper Noun	Pronoun
1.	president		
2.		San Francisco	
3.			her
4.		India	
5.		Mongols	
6.	singer		
7.			it
8.			they

D Write a sentence using each noun. Include a pronoun in at least one of your sentences. Label each noun and pronoun as a *subject* or *object.*

1. chief

   _____

2. Asia

   _____

3. weapons

   _____

4. leadership

   _____

Reviewing Verbs

⭐ **Verbs** are words that express action or a state of being. An action verb can express a physical or mental action. A state-of-being verb shows that something exists; it is always a form of the verb *to be*.

> **Action verbs:** swim, soar, creep, say, have, think, know, wonder, seem
> **State-of-being verbs:** am, is, are, was, were, has been, had been, will be, shall be, would be

Note: *To be* verbs often combine with, or "help," action verbs, as in the verb phrases *will be swimming, is going,* and *had been thinking.*

An action verb can be either **transitive** or **intransitive** based on how it is used in the sentence. A transitive verb has a direct object, which receives the action of the verb. If the verb does not need an object to complete its meaning, it is intransitive. To know if the verb is transitive, ask *What?* or *Whom?* after the verb.

> **Transitive verbs:** Darcy sang a song. (*Sang what?* Sang the song.)
> The eagle saw me. (*Saw whom?* Saw me.)
> **Intransitive verbs:** Darcy sang loudly.
> The eagle flew over the trees. (The words after the intransitive verbs tell *how* or *where.*)

 A **Circle the verb or verbs in each sentence.**

1. When I study ancient history, I feel like a time traveler.

2. Prehistory refers to the time before people began to write.

3. Archaeology is the scientific study of things that remain from human activity in the past.

4. These remains include things such as the ruins of buildings, stone tools, and even human bones.

5. Around 3000 B.C., writing developed in the Middle Eastern land of Mesopotamia.

6. Many written materials exist for archaeologists to study.

7. Scrolls, stone tablets, and wall inscriptions are three kinds of ancient writing.

8. In many later cultures, people produced maps, letters, documents, and books.

   Advantage Grammar Grade 7 © 2005 Creative Teaching Press

B Read each pair of sentences. One has a transitive verb; the other has an intransitive verb. Place a checkmark (✓) next to the sentence with a transitive verb.

1. a. _____ Martina read aloud to her father.

    b. _____ Martina read the chapter on ancient Japan.

2. a. _____ Samurai warriors carried long swords.

    b. _____ They carried on bravely from battle to battle.

3. a. _____ Some samurai served faithfully as officials in the provinces.

    b. _____ The servants served tea to the respected officials.

4. a. _____ The warriors lived away from the court at Kyoto.

    b. _____ They lived lives marked by discipline and courage.

5. a. _____ The exhibit of samurai armor held our attention.

    b. _____ The speaker held on tight to the heavy sword.

6. a. _____ The Mongols threatened Japan in the late 1200s.

    b. _____ They threatened by attacking from Korea across the Sea of Japan.

7. a. _____ After much fighting, a great storm rolled across the sea.

    b. _____ The wind and rains rolled the Mongol ships on their sides.

8. a. _____ The storm stopped the Mongol invasion of Japan.

    b. _____ We stopped briefly to look at a painting of the battle.

C Answer each question in a complete sentence. Underline all the action verbs or state-of-being verbs in your sentence.

1. How did you get to school this morning? _____

    _____

2. What is the most interesting thing you have learned today? _____

    _____

3. What have you been thinking about in the past hour? _____

    _____

4. Will you be at school tomorrow? _____

    _____

Using Negatives

LESSON

3

ANCIENT
CIVILIZATIONS
OF ASIA

⭐ **Negative words**, such as *not* and *never*, change the meaning of a verb. The verb tells what the action is; adding a negative word changes the meaning to the opposite.

I like computer games.   I do **not** like computer games.

Here are some common negative words:

not, nobody, none, nothing, hardly, can't, doesn't, won't, isn't, aren't

To be clear and correct, use only one negative word in a sentence.

Double negative (incorrect)	**Corrected**
He <u>hardly</u> <u>never</u> eats lunch out.	He <u>hardly</u> ever eats lunch out.
It <u>doesn't</u> make <u>no</u> difference.	It <u>doesn't</u> make any difference.
<u>Can't</u> <u>nobody</u> hear me?	<u>Can't</u> anybody hear me?
	Can <u>nobody</u> hear me?
There is <u>not</u> <u>nothing</u> to do.	There is <u>nothing</u> to do.
	There <u>isn't</u> anything to do.
We <u>won't</u> <u>never</u> get there.	We <u>won't</u> ever get there.
	We will <u>never</u> get there.

To correct a double negative, replace one of the negative words with a positive word, or take away a negative word.

A Circle the word that correctly completes each sentence.

1. In the distance you (can, can't) barely see a tiny tower on top of the mountain.

2. Won't (anybody, nobody) come with me to see the movie *Shogun*?

3. There was barely (nobody, anybody) in the theater when we arrived.

4. The Mongols never used (no, a) written language.

5. Wasn't there (nothing, anything) the Chinese could do to stop the Mongol invaders?

6. None of us (ever, never) guessed that riding horses well was so important in battle.

    Advantage Grammar Grade 7 © 2005 Creative Teaching Press

B Read each sentence. If the sentence is correct, write *Correct* on the line. If it is incorrect, rewrite the sentence so that it uses negative words correctly.

1. This book doesn't contain any information on ancient Japan. _____

_____

2. Sam hardly has no energy to attend his kung fu class. _____

_____

3. Isn't nobody going to give a report on the samurai? _____

_____

4. It won't make no difference if they are five minutes late. _____

_____

5. We won't have no time to visit the Zen garden at the museum. _____

_____

6. I've never seen no Japanese tea ceremony before. _____

_____

7. No one in the class had never heard of Kublai Khan before. _____

_____

8. We will never finish this time line of the Mongol Empire if we don't start soon.

_____

C Select four of the phrases from the box. For each one, write a sentence about personal experiences, current events, or interesting things you have learned in social studies.

isn't anything	nobody was
any difference	hardly ever
none of us	will never

_____

_____

_____

_____

Name _____

Commas and Semicolons

⭐ Both **commas** and **semicolons** can be used in compound sentences to join two independent clauses. Use a comma when the clauses are joined by a conjunction such as *and, but, or, nor, yet, so,* or *for.* The comma falls before the conjunction.

> Mountains and hills cover most of Japan, and it is surrounded by the sea.

Use a semicolon to join two closely related independent clauses when they are not joined by a coordinating conjunction.

> Mountains and hills cover most of Japan; less than 20 percent of the land can be used for farming.

A semicolon is also used when a conjunction such as *therefore, however, thus,* or *then* joins the two clauses.

> Hokkaido is the northernmost island; then, moving south, comes Honshu, Shikoku, and Kyushu.

A Add a semicolon in the correct place in each sentence.

1. As an island, Japan was isolated from the world thus, it developed with little influence from other countries except China.

2. Japan is located on a very unstable part of the earth's crust therefore earthquakes are common there.

3. Typhoons are also frequent in Japan these are coastal storms with tree-bending winds and heavy rains.

4. For thousands of years, the sea has been Japan's greatest resource it has provided food and helped to shield the island from invasion.

5. A Japanese myth describes how the world began two sky gods decided to create the islands of Japan by dipping a jeweled spear into the ocean.

6. Some of the earliest inhabitants of Japan were the Jomon they probably came from Korea.

7. Early peoples believed in the power of spirits these spirits were called kami.

8. The Sun Goddess was the most powerful of the kami Japan's first emperor claimed to be descended from the Sun Goddess.

B **Decide whether each sentence requires a comma or a semicolon. Add the appropriate punctuation mark to each sentence.**

1. Hunter-gatherers lived in Japan in prehistoric times and the Ainu people of northern Japan may be related to them.

2. The Jomon developed a complex culture they used irrigation to create wet fields where they cultivated rice.

3. The next civilization, the Yayoi, was called the "tomb culture" for the Yayoi built huge graves.

4. The graves contained small clay figures of soldiers and horses these objects suggest that the Yayoi took part in wars and respected warriors.

5. Japan is an island but one of its main religions, Buddhism, comes from China.

6. Japan's ruler in the 600s, Prince Shotoku, welcomed Buddhist priests they helped introduce the Chinese language and arts in Japan.

7. After Shotoku's death, government leaders introduced Chinese-style reforms all land was made the property of the emperor.

8. These reforms reduced the power of the clan leaders however, the lives of everyday peasants did not change much.

C **Write a paragraph about the early history of Japan. Include at least two compound sentences in which you join the main clauses with a comma or semicolon. Remember that clauses joined by a semicolon should be closely related in content.**

_____

_____

_____

_____

_____

_____

_____

Name _____

Adjectives and Adverbs with Inflected Endings

5

ANCIENT
CIVILIZATIONS
OF ASIA

★ When adjectives and adverbs are used to compare things, their word endings can change. In comparisons that show a *greater* quality of something, the ending *-er* is used to compare two things and *-est* to compare three or more things.

Example	Degree of Comparison
He is wearing *white* shoes.	Positive
His shoes are *whiter* than mine.	Comparative
He has the *whitest* shoes on the team.	Superlative

Most adjectives of one or two syllables, and adverbs of one syllable, add *-er* for the comparative and *-est* for the superlative. If the word ends in *-y*, it is changed to an *i* before adding the suffix. In some words, the final consonant, if single, is doubled before adding the suffix.

Positive	Comparative	Superlative
tall	taller	tallest
happy	happier	happiest
soon	sooner	soonest
red	redder	reddest

A Complete the chart by writing the correct form of the word at the left.

	Comparative	Superlative
1. cheap	_____	_____
2. tough	_____	_____
3. sturdy	_____	_____
4. dark	_____	_____
5. friendly	_____	_____
6. soon	_____	_____
7. deadly	_____	_____
8. free	_____	_____
9. narrow	_____	_____
10. tasty	_____	_____
11. late	_____	_____
12. hearty	_____	_____

B **Write the correctly spelled form of the word to complete each sentence.**

1. (safe) Japan was _____ from invasion than China because it was not on the mainland.

2. (brave) One Chinese soldier distinguished himself as the _____ of all.

3. (early) The Han Dynasty in China was _____ than the Tang Dynasty.

4. (soon) Which of the three projects will be completed _____ ?

5. (blue) The palace was a brilliant white under the _____ sky I have ever seen.

6. (angry) The emperor could not have been _____ when he received the news.

7. (long) The Great Wall of China is _____ than many rivers.

8. (worthy) Many people consider Li Bo, who lived during the Tang Dynasty, to be China's _____ poet.

9. (few) This grave contained _____ clay figurines than the other one.

10. (plain) The _____ of the four temples is located in the Himalayas.

11. (costly) This palace was the _____ one ever built at that time.

12. (near) Of the three countries, India is _____ to the equator.

13. (sad) When their beloved pet died, the empress was sad, but her daughter was even _____ .

14. (old) This statue of Buddha, from about 300 A.D., is _____ than that one.

Improving Word Choice

6

ANCIENT
CIVILIZATIONS
OF ASIA

⭐ When you reread a paragraph you have drafted, look for vague, dull, or inappropriate words. Replace them with more precise, vivid, or more appropriate words.

Yesterday, I went to a *really cool* Zen garden at the Museum of Japanese Culture. This is not a garden of flowers but a garden of rocks. The *Japanese religion* teaches that people are part of nature. For this reason, Japanese gardeners use nature to *do* art. The garden has just a few rocks. They are arranged to look like *little* mountains in a *scene*. The rocks are surrounded by sand raked in *a groovy way*. A Zen garden is a *special* place for *thinking*.

Here is a revised paragraph with better word choices. The replacement words, and some new ones, are more specific and colorful. In a few cases, the writer chose a more formal word for the report.

Yesterday, I went to a *beautiful* Zen garden at the Museum of Japanese Culture. This is not a garden of flowers but a garden of rocks. *Buddhism* teaches that people are part of nature. For this reason, Japanese gardeners use nature to *create* art. The garden has just a few large rocks. They are arranged to look like *tiny* mountains in a *natural scene*. The rocks are surrounded by sand raked into *neat patterns*. A Zen garden is a *quiet and peaceful* place for *meditation*.

A Write each new word choice that appears in the revised paragraph. Then place a check mark in one or more columns to explain why the new choice is better.

Word choice		Replacement word is . . .		
In first draft	In revision	more colorful	more precise	more appropriate
really cool				
Japanese religion				
do				
little				
scene				
a groovy way				
special				
thinking				

Advantage Grammar Grade 7 © 2005 Creative Teaching Press

B Rewrite the paragraph below. As you do, look for places where you could use more specific and vivid words to make the paragraph clearer and more interesting.

The samurai of Japan were the fighters of medieval Japan. They were similar to knights in medieval Europe. Both had horses and had armor. The samurai's armor was made up of many small plates of steel brought together with leather strips. Knights, on the other hand, wore armor made of large curved hunks of steel. Both samurai and knights swore loyalty to a lord and started their training while they were little. Both were parts of a warrior class that had a special code of doing.

_____

_____

_____

_____

C Complete the chart. Write each word that you replaced and the new word you chose in your revised paragraph. Then place a check in one or more columns to explain why the new word choice is better.

Word choice		Replacement word is . . .		
In first draft	In revision	more colorful	more precise	more appropriate

Name _____

Editing Your Work

⭐ Editing your work is an important step in the writing process. Many tests ask you to show what you know about editing.

A **Sonia wrote a report about the Great Wall of China. Help her revise and edit her work. Read the report. Then answer the questions that follow.**

The Great Wall of China

1) The Chinese emperors were determined to keep out invaders. 2) They built an awesome wall known as the great wall of China. 3) This long wall runs from east to west along the northern line of China. 4) The wall was made of stone. 5) In addition, most parts of the wall were thirty feet high, that's about as tall as a two-story house. 6) The watchtowers along the wall were even taller.

7) China's first ruler came up with the idea for the project. 8) This was back around 200 B.C. 9) He decided to connect some shorter walls that already existed to defend China's border. 10) The Great Wall today is about 4,000 miles long however, that includes many branches.

1. Which words in sentence 2 should be capitalized? Why? _____

_____

2. Rewrite sentence 3, replacing a vague word with a more precise word.

_____

3. What is the verb in sentence 3? Is it transitive or intransitive? How do you know? _____

_____

4. How would you correct the punctuation error in sentence 5? _____

5. In sentence 7, why would *emperor* be a better word choice than *ruler*? Why?

_____

6. Rewrite sentence 10, using correct punctuation between the two main clauses.

_____

B **Continuing reading and editing Sonia's report.**

      1) Building the Great Wall was a huge project. 2) It required hundreds of thousands of workers. 3) Most of them were ordered to do the work they did not volunteer. 4) Many of the workers were soldiers. 5) The emperor also got rid of his personal enemies by sending them to work on distant parts of the wall. 6) The work was difficult, and the living conditions were harsh. 7) As a result, thousands of laborers died.

      8) Many workers must have thought, "This wall won't never be finished." 9) Generation after generation extended the wall. 10) In the 1400s and 1500s, much of the wall was rebuilt to make it sturder. 11) It is still the longest structure on Earth!

1. Sentence 3 has a punctuation error. Rewrite the sentence correctly.

_____

_____

2. In sentence 5, the pronoun *them* is used in place of what word?

_____

3. Which noun is the direct object in sentence 9?

_____

4. Why is a comma appropriate for separating the clauses in sentence 6?

_____

_____

5. Are the verbs in sentence 6 action verbs or state-of-being verbs?

_____

6. Rewrite sentence 8 to correct the double negative.

_____

_____

7. Circle the word in sentence 10 that is misspelled. Write the correct spelling.

_____

Name _____

Take a Test Drive

Fill in the bubble beside the correct answer.

Lamont wrote an essay about the time when the Mongols ruled China. Help him edit his essay. Read the essay, and answer the following questions.

1) The Mongols were the first outsiders to rule China. 2) They conquered northern China in the early 1200s. 3) Under leader Genghis Khan, the Mongol horsemen made many surprise attacks along the Chinese frontier. 4) They used catapults and gunpow-der bombs to damage northern cities. 5) The Chinese armies had few horses and did not ride as well as the Mongols therefore, they could not resist the invaders.

6) Kublai Khan, the next Mongol ruler, moved his capital to Beijing in northern China. 7) He wanted to strengthen his rule, so he adopted some of the Chinese tradi-tions of government. 8) For example, he declared himself emperor and Son of Heaven, like other Chinese rulers. 9) Eventually, Kublai Khan conquered southern China as well.

1. Which statement about sentence 1 is true.
   Ⓐ *Mongols* is a common noun.
   Ⓑ The word *were* is a state-of-being verb.
   Ⓒ It is incorrectly punctuated.
   Ⓓ It shows poor word choice.

2. What punctuation is missing in sentence *5*?
   Ⓕ a comma before *therefore*   Ⓗ a semicolon before *therefore*
   Ⓖ a comma after *ride*   Ⓙ a semicolon after *armies*

3. Which statement is true?
   Ⓐ Sentence 5 contains a double negative.
   Ⓑ Sentence 6 contains an intransitive verb.
   Ⓒ Sentence 7 is correctly punctuated.
   Ⓓ The subject of sentence 9 is a pronoun.

4. Which statement accurately describes the second paragraph?
   Ⓕ The writer used precise action verbs.
   Ⓖ The writer used only intransitive verbs.
   Ⓗ The writer used only pronouns as subjects.
   Ⓙ The writer used a semicolon incorrectly.

Name _____

Debra wrote an essay about the Ming Dynasty in China. Read the next paragraph, and answer the questions below to help her make revisions and corrections.

1) For a long time, there wasn't nothing the Chinese could do about having a Mongol ruler. 2) After about a hundred years, though, the Chinese rebelled against the outsiders. 3) The rebel leader founded the Ming Dynasty. 4) The Ming emperors were harshier than previous rulers. 5) They created a secret police force to spy on people. 6) They accused many thousands of people of treason or corruption; and these people were executed.

7) There was also a positive side to Ming rule. 8) The Ming emperors built a grand new capital at Beijing. 9) They also sent a guy named Zheng Ho to discover all he could about the Middle East and the east coast of Africa.

5. What error does sentence 1 contain?
Ⓐ incorrect capitalization
Ⓑ incorrect punctuation
Ⓒ a double negative
Ⓓ a misspelled word

6. How should sentence 4 be corrected?
Ⓕ Lowercase the word *Ming*.
Ⓖ Spell the word *harshier* correctly as *harsher*.
Ⓗ Capitalize the word *emperors*.
Ⓙ Change the word *rulers* to *kings*.

7. What change should be made in sentence 6?
Ⓐ Change the semicolon to a comma.
Ⓑ Capitalize *and*.
Ⓒ Change *executed* to *hurt*.
Ⓓ Remove the semicolon.

8. Which would be the best choice to replace *a guy* in sentence 9?
Ⓕ a friend
Ⓖ a soldier
Ⓗ an explorer
Ⓙ a person

LESSON 9

BEYOND THE EARTH

Reviewing Adverbs and Adjectives

 Adverbs and adjectives are both modifiers. They make the meaning of another word more specific. **Adjectives** add meaning to nouns and pronouns. They usually precede the word they describe. They can also follow a linking verb, such as *was* or *seems*.

A **bright** moon shone in the sky. The moon was **full**.

The dog shivered under the **bright waxing January** moon.

Adverbs modify verbs, adjectives, and other adverbs.

The owl flew **silently**. The sky is **very** clear. Speak **more** slowly.

They often tell where, when, how, or how much. The word *not* is also considered an adverb.

The moon rose **there** at 9 p.m.   The moon seemed to rise **quickly**.

The moon rose **early**.   The moon did **not** rise.

A **Draw an arrow from the adjective to the noun it modifies.**

1. As Earth travels through space, the moon is a constant companion.

2. Once a month, the moon makes a complete journey around Earth.

3. The moon looks bright to us because it reflects light from the sun.

4. When the sun shines on the whole side of the moon facing us, the moon looks full.

5. For much of the month, Earth blocks some or all of the powerful light from the sun.

6. You can see the changing shape of the moon from night to night.

7. The different shapes are called phases.

8. When Earth casts a large shadow on the moon, you see a crescent moon.

   Advantage Grammar Grade 7 © 2005 Creative Teaching Press

B Draw an arrow from each adverb to the word it modifies. Below the line, label the modified word as a verb (v), adjective (adj), or adverb (adv).

1. It was September 23, 1882, a very beautiful fall day in the Northern Hemisphere.

2. The moon was rising conveniently, just as the sun was setting.

3. Gabriel had been working extremely hard to harvest the corn.

4. With the extra light from the moon, he happily continued his work.

5. Even today, people call the full moon in September the Harvest Moon.

C Read each word. Decide if it is an adjective or an adverb. Write it under the correct heading. Some words can be both an adjective and an abverb.

very	not	smiley	high	quickly
rarely	modern	original	extremely	quite
serious	few	every	energetic	late
truly	southern	cool	tasty	almost

Adjectives

_____

_____

_____

_____

_____

_____

Adverbs

_____

_____

_____

_____

_____

_____

LESSON

10

BEYOND THE EARTH

Reviewing Prepositions and Conjunctions

⭐ Prepositions and conjunctions are linkers. Conjunctions link words or groups of words, including whole clauses.

> The astronaut orbited Earth **and** the moon.
> We looked at pictures of Mercury, Venus, **and** Mars.
> The days are shorter now, **and** the weather is colder.
> The sun was setting, **so** we went home.

Notice that a comma is used before *and* in a series and before a conjunction that joins two clauses. Some of the most common conjunctions are *and, but, or, nor, so, yet,* and *for.*

Prepositions begin phrases that usually end with a noun or pronoun. They show how the noun or pronoun is related to other words in the sentence. Prepositional phrases often give information about time, place, and condition.

> We saw the solar eclipse **at noon**.
> The telescope sits **on a tripod**.
> Everyone was present **except Miguel**.

Some common prepositions are *on, for, in, of, by, about, to, toward, from, after, with,* and *until.*

A In each sentence, identify the underlined word as a conjunction *(C)* or a preposition *(P)*. Write the correct letter on the line.

_____ **1.** I am looking in the right direction, <u>but</u> I can't find the North Star.

_____ **2.** How far is the moon <u>from</u> Earth?

_____ **3.** Do you think people will ever live <u>on</u> the moon?

_____ **4.** <u>After</u> the solar eclipse, we removed our special sunglasses.

_____ **5.** It was not Jeff <u>but</u> Jamal who knew the answer.

_____ **6.** This chapter describes comets, meteors, <u>and</u> asteroids.

_____ **7.** The comet was not very large, <u>nor</u> did it have a long tail.

_____ **8.** Even <u>with</u> the naked eye, you can see craters on the moon's surface.

 Advantage Grammar Grade 7 © 2005 Creative Teaching Press

B Here are some other common prepositions. Choose six of the prepositions, and write a short sentence using each one.

into	during	instead of	until
between	through	without	except

1. _____

2. _____

3. _____

4. _____

5. _____

6. _____

C Combine the sentences into one sentence using the appropriate conjunction from the list. Be sure to insert commas where they are needed.

or   and   but   so

1. Comets are made of ice. Comets are made of stones. Comets are made of dust. Comets are made of lumps of metal.

_____

_____

2. Asteroids are small objects made of rock. "Small" can mean 600 miles across.

_____

_____

3. We had forgotten our special sunglasses. We did not look directly at the solar eclipse.

_____

_____

4. I will do a science project on comets. I will do a science project on asteroids.

_____

_____

LESSON

BEYOND THE EARTH

Placing Modifiers Correctly

 A **modifier** describes, clarifies, or gives more detail about a part of speech. A modifier can be a word, sentence, or clause. To make sure that the meaning of a sentence is clear, always place modifiers close to the thing you want them to modify. Notice how the placement of the word *tomorrow* in these two sentences changes the meaning:

> I will ask Mike to go to the movie tomorrow.
> Tomorrow, I will ask Mike to go to the movie.

Placing modifying phrases and clauses correctly is also important, as this example shows:

> I put the pie in the refrigerator, which we ate the next day.

This sentence contains a *misplaced modifier*. Another common error with modifiers is the *dangling modifier*. In this case, the word or words that the modifier refers to are missing from the sentence.

> Looking out the window, the sun was setting.

Both misplaced and dangling modifiers can lead to confusion. To correct them, express the noun the modifier describes, move the modifier within the sentence, or rewrite the sentence.

> I put the pie, which we ate the next day, in the refrigerator.
> Looking out the window, I saw that the sun was beginning to set.
> When I looked out the window, I saw that the sun was setting.

A **Read each sentence. Underline the misplaced or dangling modifier. It may be a word, phrase, or clause. Then identify the type of modifier.**

1. Although tired, the meteor shower was so spectacular that we stayed up till 1 a.m.

   misplaced   dangling

2. To be considered among the top science students, your project must look professional.

   misplaced   dangling

3. We gave our teacher a poster showing Earth from outer space in a black frame.

   misplaced   dangling

     Advantage Grammar Grade 7 © 2005 Creative Teaching Press

B **Rewrite each sentence to correct the dangling modifier.**

1. Before going home, a full moon had risen over the treetops.

_____

2. Although noisy and excited, the speaker ignored the students.

_____

3. Staying out to look at the winter sky, my ears nearly froze.

_____

4. Looking out the car window, the lunar eclipse was just beginning.

_____

5. Stepping inside the air and space museum, a guide met the students.

_____

C **Rewrite each sentence to correct the misplaced modifier.**

1. We only bought a few souvenirs when we went to the space center.

_____

2. Arnie picked up the guide to stars that his father had given him with a sigh.

_____

3. The science editor he had written to after much deliberation rejected his article.

_____

4. We almost went to the end of the dirt road before we set up the telescope.

_____

5. Several of us spotted the Sea of Tranquility with our binoculars on the moon.

_____

Parentheses and Brackets

12

BEYOND THE
EARTH

⭐ Parentheses set off information that is not part of the main statement in a sentence. They may enclose a word, a phrase, a clause, or even a whole sentence. Parentheses are always used in pairs.

> This meteorite weighs only 3 ounces (57 grams).
> One small meteorite (to my surprise) weighed almost a pound.
> Brad's report on meteorites (he gave it on Tuesday) was very interesting.

If a punctuation mark follows the item in parentheses, it falls outside the closing parenthesis.

> Please hand me that meteorite (the one that looks like a peanut).
> I met with Ms. Gorsick (my advisor), and then I went home.

Brackets have the same function as parentheses, but they are used mainly in two situations:

> * Inside parentheses to enclose a comment or extra information
>   An Italian astronomer (Giuseppe Piazzi [1746–1826]) discovered the first asteroid.

> * In a quotation to enclose a clarification or comment
>   Professor Updike said, "In March of that year [1999], I spent many hours at the observatory."

A Read each sentence. If the parentheses or brackets are used correctly, write **C** on the line. If they are used incorrectly, write **I**.

_____ **1.** It was very late (past midnight) when we went out into the backyard.

_____ **2.** "The sky is falling," exclaimed my little sister Inez (she is only four.

_____ **3.** She didn't understand about meteors (an occurrence in the night sky.)

_____ **4.** I paid a lot of money [$17.95] for this new book on astronomy.

_____ **5.** The author (his picture is on the back) is G. I. Seestars.

_____ **6.** As director of the Nicholson Observatory (1995–2005), he gave many talks at the planetarium.

_____ **7.** I turned to the section on meteorites chapter 6), and I began to read.

_____ **8.** In August (especially during the second week), you can see hundreds of bright streaks in the sky.

B **Rewrite each sentence using parentheses and brackets correctly.**

1. Seestars writes, "They (the streaks) may look like falling stars, but they are really the trails of meteors."

   _____

   _____

2. Bits of rock (and also metal exist in the space between Earth and the other planets. _____

   _____

3. Bits that are closer to Earth fall toward it (and us because of gravity.

   _____

   _____

4. The particles fall very fast (at up to 150,000 miles 250,000 km per hour).

   _____

   _____

5. Friction [rubbing] with the air in Earth's atmosphere heats them up.

   _____

   _____

6. The rock bits burn up and leave a fiery trail (what we see as a meteor.)

   _____

   _____

C **Insert parentheses or brackets in each sentence where they are needed.**

1. The astronomy lecture at the planetarium is this Friday August 12, 2005.

2. On our last camping trip to the mountains we went to the Rockies, we saw a spectacular meteor shower.

3. Pike's Peak elevation 14,110 feet 4,301 meters is a great place to view the stars.

4. Professor Higgins he teaches at the local college is an expert on meteors.

LESSON

Verbs with Inflected Endings

13

BEYOND THE EARTH

⭐ Verb endings help to show the tense of a verb. With regular verbs, you often add *-s*, *-es*, or *-ing* to show the present tense and *-ed* to show the past and perfect tenses.

Present tense: he *writes*, she *wishes*, they are *walking*

Past and perfect tenses: you *wondered*, he has *noticed*, they had *feared*, it will have *landed*

Use the rules below to spell these verb forms correctly.

To add *-ed* and *-ing* correctly

If the word ends in . . .	Then . . .	Example
A consonant that follows a single vowel	Double the consonant IF the word has one syllable or is accented on the second syllable.	tap, tapped, tapping refer, referred, referring
A consonant that follows two vowels or another consonant, or if the word has two syllables with the accent on the second syllable	Do not double the final consonant.	heat, heated, heating start, started, starting depart, departed, departing
Silent *e*	Generally drop the e.	tape, taped, taping
A vowel plus *y*	Keep the y.	play, played, playing
A consonant plus *y*	Change the y to an *i* when adding *-ed*, and keep the y when adding *-ing*.	spy, spied, spying

To add *-ed* and *-ing* correctly

If the word ends in . . .	Then . . .	Example
A consonant or in a vowel plus *y*	Add *-s*.	win, wins play, plays
Any s sound (*s, sh, ch, x, z, zz*)	Add *-es*.	brush, brushes fizz, fizzes
A consonant plus *y*	Change the y to an *i*, and add *-es*.	spy, spies

A Add -s or -es to each word to form the correct form of the verb.

1. relay _____
2. push _____
3. tax _____
4. relate _____
5. refer _____
6. try _____
7. greet _____
8. sizzle _____
9. surround _____
10. deny _____

B Write the correctly spelled form of the verb to complete each sentence.

1. Last night Ursula _____ the North Star through her brother's telescope.   (view)
2. Nigel has _____ to locate the Big Dipper several times without success.   (try)
3. Lenore is _____ the book about constellations.   (renew)
4. Some people were _____ on the bike trail because the moon was so bright.   (jog)
5. The presence of clouds has _____ the telescope demonstration.   (delay)
6. The speaker _____ to two photographs of the moon as he talked.   (refer)
7. Leon and Cy had been _____ out under the stars for hours.   (sit)

Name _____

BEYOND THE EARTH

Varying Sentence Structure

⭐ You can make your paragraphs clearer and more interesting by using different types of sentences. To check for sentence variety, read your paragraphs out loud. If you notice a lot of short, choppy sentences, combine some of them to improve the flow and sharpen the meaning. If you have lots of long sentences, break them up with a few short and snappy ones. Let the information and your ear be your guide.

Here are some different types of sentences you can use.

Sentence Type	Structure	Example
Simple	One independent clause	Asteroids are small objects made of rock.
Compound	Two or more independent clauses and no subordinate clauses	Some asteroids are large, but others are small.
Complex	An independent clause and one or more subordinate clauses.	When the planets formed, some rocks were left over.

 A **Read the draft paragraph below and the revision. Then follow the directions at the top of the next page.**

Draft

There is something unusual between the planets of Mars and Jupiter. It is belt of minor planets called asteroids. Asteroids are rocks in space. There are several thousand asteroids. One of them is called Ceres. It is the largest. Its diameter is 567 miles. Ceres is as big as a small moon. Most asteroids are smaller than 10 miles in diameter. The asteroid belt also contains millions of boulders, stones, and grains of sand.

Revision

Between the planets of Mars and Jupiter lies something unusual. It is a belt of minor planets called asteroids. You can think of asteroids as rocks in space. There are thousands of them. The largest one, which is 567 miles in diameter, is called Ceres. While Ceres is as big as a small moon, most asteroids are smaller than 10 miles in diameter. The asteroid belt also contains millions of boulders, stones, and grains of sand.

Advantage Grammar Grade 7 © 2005 Creative Teaching Press

Find two places in the revision where the writer created a complex sentence from two or more simple sentences in the draft. Write the revised sentence and the sentences it replaced below.

1. Complex sentence _____

_____

Sentences replaced _____

_____

_____

2. Complex sentence _____

_____

Sentences replaced _____

_____

B **Rewrite the paragraph below. In your revision, improve the flow and meaning by using more varied sentences.**

The spacecraft *Galileo* visited two asteroids. The spacecraft was on its way to Jupiter. Asteroids are unlike planets and moons. Planets and moons are spherical. Asteroids can be lumpy. One of the asteroids near Jupiter is shaped like a potato. It is named Gaspra. It has a few small craters. These were made by meteorites. The other asteroid is named Ida. It has its own little moon.

_____

_____

_____

_____

_____

_____

_____

_____

Editing Your Work

 Editing your work is an important step in the writing process. Many tests ask you to show what you know about editing.

BEYOND THE EARTH

 Mario wrote a report about Earth and the sun. Help him revise his work. Read the paragraphs and then follow the directions.

The Sun and the Seasons

1) Did you know that Earth moves in two different ways? 2) It traveles around the sun. 3) This journey takes a year. 4) It also spins, making a complete rotation every 24 hours.

5) Earth spins like a top, but it does not stand up straight. It leans. 6) This tilt is the reason that we have seasons on Earth. 7) It also explains why day length changes in different seasons.

8) To see how, try this experiment [from the book *Earth and Sun* (1998)]. 9) You will need a 6-inch polystyrene ball, a new pencil, and a flashlight. 10) Insert the pencil through the center of the ball (to represent Earth and its axis.) 11) Then, draw a line around the ball half way between the pencil ends. 12) This line divides the ball (Earth) into northern and southern hemispheres. 13) Place the ball and the flashlight (representing the sun) on a table, with the ball on your right.

1. In sentence 1, are the words *two* and *different* adverbs or adjectives? Explain.

_____

2. Which sentence in the first paragraph contains an incorrectly spelled verb? Spell the word correctly. Then spell the past-tense form of the verb.

_____

3. Which two sentences in the third paragraph contain two errors in using parentheses or brackets? Write each sentence correctly. _____

_____

_____

_____

    Advantage Grammar Grade 7 © 2005 Creative Teaching Press

B **Continue reading Mario's essay. Help him edit the next part by answering the questions below.**

1) After dimming the room lights, the flashlight is turned on and pointed at the ball. 2) Adjust the ball so the axis (pencil) is leaning *away* from the light. 3) Notice that the sun shins directly on the southern (bottom) hemisphere. 4) It receives more heat and more hours of daylight than the northern (top hemisphere. 5) This situation represents summer in the Southern Hemisphere. 6) It also represents winter in the Northern Hemisphere.

7) Next, turn the flashlight to point left, and move the ball to the opposite (left) side of the flashlight. 8) Keep the direction of the pencil's tilt just the same. 9) Now the North Pole (top end of pencil) is toward the sun. 10) The sun lights up more of the Northern Hemisphere than the Southern Hemisphere. 11) This situation represents summer in our hemisphere, so the days are longer than the nights.

1. Revise sentence 1 to correct the dangling modifier.

_____

_____

_____

2. Sentence 3 has a spelling error. Rewrite the sentence correctly.

_____

3. In sentence 4, the closing parenthesis has been omitted. Where should it be inserted?

_____

4. Combine sentences 5 and 6 using a conjunction to make a *shorter* sentence that improves the flow.

_____

_____

_____

5. In sentence 9, what part of speech is the word *toward*? How do you know?

_____

_____

_____

Name _____

Fill in the bubble beside the correct answer.

Read Anika's essay about asteroids. Help her revise and edit her work by answering the questions that follow.

Asteroids

1) Asteroids are tiny objects in our solar system made of rock. 2) A belt of asteroids is located between the orbits of Mars and Jupiter. 3) Some of these asteroids have orbits that cross Earth's once-a-year orbit around the sun. 4) Because of this, single asteroids sometimes come very close to the earth. 5) Such objects are known as near-Earth objects [NEOs].

6) Some near asteroids have crashed into Earth. 7) A small asteroid (30 to 100 feet across) strikes Earth about once in a lifetime. 8) Such rocks are not dangerous. 9) If a very large asteroid (more than half a mile across) struck Earth, it could cause a worldwide disaster. 10) A rock this large reaches Earth about once every 100,000 years.

1. Which statement is true about sentence 1?
- Ⓐ It contains a dangling modifier.
- Ⓑ It contains a misplaced modifier.
- Ⓒ It contains a conjunction.
- Ⓓ It contains a preposition without an object.

2. In sentence 4, which word does the adverb *very* modify?
- Ⓕ come
- Ⓖ close
- Ⓗ earth
- Ⓙ to

3. How should sentence 5 be rewritten?
- Ⓐ Such objects are known as near-Earth objects [NEOs.]
- Ⓑ Such objects are known as near-Earth objects (NEOs).
- Ⓒ Such objects are known as near-Earth objects (NEOs.)
- Ⓓ Such objects are known as near-Earth objects, NEOs.

4. What type of sentence is sentence 9?
- Ⓕ simple
- Ⓖ compound
- Ⓗ complex
- Ⓙ compound-complex

Advantage Grammar Grade 7 © 2005 Creative Teaching Press

Name _____

Continue reading and editing Anika's report. Answer the questions below.

11) About 65 million years ago, during the dinosaur age, a small asteroid smashed into Earth. 12) This happened in the area of Mexico. 13) The impact blasted dirt and rock into the air, and caused fires all across Earth. 14) The heat caused a climate change that wiped out all large animals on Earth. 15) Some small animals such as mice survived, for they were able to burrow.

16) Only asteroids and comets could cause a disaster if they struck Earth. 17) About twenty meteorites fall to Earth each year. 18) They are usually small. 19) Large meteorites are rare. 20) When they strike Earth, they can cause craters a mile or more across.

5. Which verb illustrates the rule for adding *-ed* to a word ending in silent *e*?
Ⓐ smashed
Ⓑ happened
Ⓒ blasted
Ⓓ survived

6. Which phrase begins with a preposition?
Ⓕ all large animals
Ⓖ and caused fires
Ⓗ across Earth
Ⓙ able to burrow

7. What is the best way to rewrite sentences 17 and 18?
Ⓐ About twenty meteorites fall to Earth each year, and they are usually very small.
Ⓑ About twenty meteorites fall to Earth each year, so they are usually very small.
Ⓒ About twenty meteorites fall to Earth each year, for they are usually very small.
Ⓓ About twenty meteorites fall to Earth each year, but they are usually very small.

8. What part of speech is *rare* in sentence 19?
Ⓕ noun
Ⓖ adjective
Ⓗ verb
Ⓙ adverb

Types of Sentences

17

YOUR LAND,
MY LAND

★ Sentences are the basic building blocks in every kind of writing. There are four types of sentences. Each one has a different function.

Type	*Function*	*Ends with a . . .*
Declarative	Gives facts	Period
Interrogative	Asks a question	Question mark
Imperative	Gives a command or makes a request	Period
Exclamatory	Expresses strong feeling	Exclamation point

Examples
The Everglades is a wetland. (declarative)
What is a wetland? (interrogative)
Look at the alligator. (imperative)
That alligator snapped at me! (exclamatory)

If a declarative, interrogative, or imperative sentence expresses strong feeling, treat it as an exclamatory sentence.
This is terrific!   How could you!   Hey, wait for me!

A Identify each sentence as declarative (D), interrogative (I), imperative (C), or exclamatory (E).

_____ **1.** What is the fee to use this campground?

_____ **2.** The camping fees range from $10 to $20 per vehicle.

_____ **3.** Please display your camping permit on the dashboard of your vehicle.

_____ **4.** The line to get into the campground is fifty cars long!

_____ **5.** The alligator was sunning itself on a log.

_____ **6.** Do not feed the alligators.

_____ **7.** The signs repeatedly warn visitors not to feed any wildlife.

_____ **8.** This camping spot is perfect!

_____ **9.** We have a fine view of the lake and the mountains beyond.

_____ **10.** Can we tell stories around the campfire later?

B Add the correct ending punctuation to each sentence.

1. Look at a map of Florida to locate Everglades National Park

2. Did you know that there is very little dry land in the Everglades

3. Because the Everglades is a wetland, you travel through it by boat

4. Much of the park looks like a sea of grass

5. Here and there, jungle-like stands of trees grow on little raised islands

6. Herons, egrets, and other wading birds find plenty of food in the calm water

7. The park is home to several endangered animals, such as the manatee, crocodile, and Florida panther

8. Wow That hawk just snatched a fish

9. Can you tell me how to get to Gumbo Limbo Trail

10. Please help save this fragile ecosystem

C Use the information in the sentence provided to write three sentences of different types. You can add or subtract words, but keep the topic the same.

Example: Please do not feed the raccoons.
(declarative) We did not feed the raccoons.
(interrogative) Did you feed the baby raccoon?
(exclamatory) They fed the raccoons apple pie!

1. You can usually see birds such as ospreys and pelicans here.
(interrogative) _____
(exclamatory) _____
(imperative) _____

2. What an awesome set of teeth that alligator has!
(declarative) _____
(interrogative) _____
(imperative) _____

3. Take the self-guided, half-mile walk to Nine Mile Pond.
(exclamatory) _____
(declarative) _____
(interrogative) _____

L E S S O N

**YOUR LAND,
MY LAND**

Using the Perfect Tenses

 The simple tenses express past, present, and future. The **perfect tenses** also express past, present, and future, but they refer to actions that take place *over time*.

Each of the three perfect tenses uses a form of the helping verb *to have*. The form depends on whether the subject is *I, you, he/she/it, we,* or *they*.

Singular:	I have	you have	he/she/it has
Plural:	we have	you have	they have

Present perfect shows that an action or condition has been completed at the present time or is still going on.

   We *have waited* a long time.   (completed as of now)

   We *have been waiting* a long time.   (still going on)

Past perfect shows that an action will be completed before a stated or known time in the past. It describes an action "two steps back."

   Before the storm arrived, she *had climbed* to the top of the hill.
   (past event)   (further in the past)

Future perfect shows that an action will be completed before a stated or known time in the future.

   By the time the storm arrives, they *will have finished* their hike.
   (future event)   (sooner in the future)

A Underline the present-perfect tense of the verb in each sentence. Then circle one of the words below the sentence to indicate whether the action has now been completed or is continuing in the present.

1. Ruben has written a letter to his uncle about our trip.

   completed   continuing

2. We have lived near Rocky Mountain National Park for ten years.

   completed   continuing

3. The lake has been too cold for swimming.

   completed   continuing

  Advantage Grammar Grade 7 © 2005 Creative Teaching Press

B Circle the form of the verb that correctly completes each sentence.

1. By the time we get to the top of the mountain, the sun (will have set, had set).

2. We took a shower after we (had soaked, will have soaked) in the hot springs.

3. The volcano (had been smoking, will have been smoking) for months before it erupted.

4. We did not go swimming because the weather (will have turned, had turned) cold.

5. They (had been hiking, will have been hiking) along the trail for about an hour, when they met a large moose.

C Complete each sentence by writing the appropriate form of the verb in parentheses.

Use the present-perfect, past-perfect, or future-perfect tense as needed.

1. By the time Anna arrived at the cabin, Robin and Henry _____ . (leave)

2. On every day of our car trip, we _____ to books-on-tape. (listen)

3. They were tired the next day because they _____ up past midnight. (stay)

4. By the end of the hike, the Boy Scouts _____ nine miles. (cover)

5. Our family chose Acadia National Park for a vacation because we _____ about it from a friend. (hear)

6. Only a few pioneers came to the Badlands in the 1800s, but humans _____ there for several thousand years. (live)

7. Gina _____ to Badlands National Park every summer since she was six. (come)

8. Before Mr. Cruz became a park ranger, he _____ a fish hatchery. (own)

Name _____

Using Subordinate Clauses as Adjectives

19

YOUR LAND,
MY LAND

★ Some sentences have a main clause and a subordinate clause. The main clause states the most important idea in the sentence and can stand by itself. The **subordinate clause** is less important and cannot stand alone. It depends on the main clause to complete its meaning.

We saw sandstone arches at Arches National Park, which is located in Utah.
        (main clause)   (subordinate clause)

In this sentence, the subordinate clause is used as an adjective. It describes the noun *Park*. Adjective clauses are always connected to the main clause by a relative pronoun such as *who, whom, whose, which,* or *that*.

Relative clauses may contain essential or nonessential information. Use commas to set off only nonessential clauses.

The woman who is wearing a red parka is my mom. (essential)
My mom, who is wearing a red parka, loves to go camping. (nonessential)

A **Underline the subordinate clause in each sentence. Then draw an arrow from the clause to the noun or pronoun it modifies.**

1. The formations that we saw are made of soft red sandstone.

2. The park, which is in southern Utah, has many arches, spires, and domes of rock.

3. People who take the scenic drive to Devil's Garden pass through the heart of the park.

4. The ranger who is leading the hike through Fiery Furnace is named Fred Dogood.

5. Ranger Dogood, whom we met on the trail, asked if we had enough water.

6. Each year, the park receives almost a million visitors, who enjoy the stunning scenery.

7. The dry, rocky land, which looks indestructible, is actually a fragile desert ecosystem.

                                            Advantage Grammar Grade 7 © 2005 Creative Teaching Press

Name _____

B Read each sentence containing a subordinate clause. If the clause is nonessential, add commas to set it off from the main clause. If the clause is essential, write *Essential* on the line.

1. The park which was established in 1971 has more than 2,000 natural arches.
   _____

2. The arch that is most famous is called Delicate Arch. _____

3. The colorful rocks that we see today were once part of a huge sea.
   _____

4. Forces in the earth's crust which became unstable tilted and lifted up the beds of sand. _____

5. Frost, snow, and rain eroded the soft rock which has taken on fantastic shapes as a result. _____

6. The formations whose colors include pink, lavender, and orange are still eroding. _____

7. Coyotes, bobcats, and foxes which come out at night are native to the area.
   _____

8. Among the birds that live in the park are mountain bluebirds and red-tailed hawks. _____

C Combine the sentences in each pair using a relative pronoun to show subordination. Remember to set off nonessential clauses with commas.

Example: The road is four miles long. It leads to the Double Arch.
             The road, which is four miles long, leads to the Double Arch.

1. The hike is led by a naturalist. The hike starts at sunrise.
   _____

2. The author Edward Abbey lived in the park. He wrote a book called *Desert Solitaire.* _____
   _____

3. One rock formation is Skyline Arch. Jane likes this formation best.
   _____

Using Colons

20

YOUR LAND,
MY LAND

⭐ The colon is used to introduce. It can introduce a list, a long quotation, or a word, phrase, or statement that you want to emphasize. It often follows phrases such as *the following* or *as follows.*

Be sure to pack the following items: sunglasses, sunscreen, and a first aid kit.

Colons also act as separators. Use a colon to separate the following:

* The greeting and body of a letter in a business letter
  Dear Mr. McDougle:
  We are taking a survey of park visitors.

* Hours and minutes when writing time
  We got to the lodge at 8:00 in the evening.

* The title and subtitle of a book
  Sandra is reading *Yellowstone National Park: Western Wonderland.*

A **Add a colon to each sentence where it is needed.**

1. This road takes you past several geysers Grand Geyser, Lone Star Geyser, and Old Faithful.

2. At precisely 7 52 a.m., Old Faithful sent a great plume of water one hundred feet into the air.

3. Along the roadside, Belinda saw many signs with these words Deer Crossing.

4. There were five young people on the bicycle tour Donny, Martin, Liz, Kiesha, and Tom.

5. Remember Always stay on the marked trails.

6. The ranger had this comment as we approached Old Faithful "Enjoy the show from the safety of the boardwalk."

7. My uncle, a photographer, gave me some good advice When taking pictures of geysers, always use a fast shutter speed.

8. During our stay in Yellowstone, we saw the following animals bison, bighorn sheep, beavers, mink, and moose.

9. Jan read aloud from the booklet *Observing Wildlife Do's* and *Don'ts.*

10. The park offers many conveniences post offices, photo shops, boat rentals, and bus tours.

 Advantage Grammar Grade 7 © 2005 Creative Teaching Press

B Add colons where they are needed in this business letter that Micah wrote to the public services director at the state highway department.

Dear Ms. Jimenez

I have organized a group of students at Public School 123 who are concerned about litter. We would like to volunteer for the Adopt-a-Highway program. Mr. Green, our social studies teacher, is our advisor. We can work from 8 00 to 12 00 a.m. or 12 00 to 4 00 p.m. on any Saturday in September. From your Web site, we know that you will provide bags and tools for us to use as well as bright yellow safety vests for us to wear.

Currently, the following students have agreed to pick up litter Ryan Dice, Steve Grosnik, Charlene Wu, Grace Miller, Darlene Gregg, and me. Please let me know by August 20 which day and time we should plan on working.

Sincerely,

Micah Burnett

C Write a reply from Ms. Jimenez to Micah's letter. Use at least three colons in the letter.

_____

_____

_____

_____

_____

_____

_____

_____

_____

_____

LESSON

YOUR LAND, MY LAND

Prefixes

⭐ A prefix is a letter or group of letters added to the beginning of a word to change its meaning. When adding a prefix to a word, do not change the spelling of the original word.

un + necessary = unnecessary

mis + spell = misspell

co + exist = coexist

Here are some common prefixes and how they change the meaning of a word.

Prefix	Meaning	Example
dis-	opposite	disallow (not allow)
in-, il-, im-, ir-	not, without	incorrect (not correct)
mis-	bad, wrongly	misdeed (bad deed)
non-	not, without	nonstop (without stopping)
over-	too much, beyond	overdo (do too much)
post-	after	postgame (after the game)
pre-	before	preview (view before)
re-	again	rewrite (write again)
sub-	under, less than	understate (state less than)
un-	not	unsure (not sure)

 Complete each sentence by circling the correctly spelled word in parentheses.

1. The three legs of the trail form an (irregular, iregular) triangle.

2. Juan left a note for us under a rock, but the handwriting was (ilegible, illegible).

3. The children's misbehavior did not go (unoticed, unnoticed) by the adults.

4. Trevor was (disatisfied, dissatisfied) with how the picture turned out.

5. You can (reenter, renter) the park on Sunrise Road.

6. The campsite was (overun, overrun) with chipmunks.

7. As it turned out, the extra water we carried was (uneeded, unneeded).

8. I think the ranger (misstated, mistated) the elevation of Mount McKinley.

 Advantage Grammar Grade 7 © 2005 Creative Teaching Press

B Add the prefix to each word to spell a new word. Use the prefix to state the meaning of the new word.

	New Word	Meaning
1. im + patient	_____	_____
2. ir + responsible	_____	_____
3. pre + pay	_____	_____
4. non + sense	_____	_____
5. mis + calculate	_____	_____
6. over + react	_____	_____
7. un + certain	_____	_____
8. re + arrange	_____	_____
9. over + eat	_____	_____
10. im + possible	_____	_____
11. re + assemble	_____	_____
12. sub + title	_____	_____
13. un + comfortable	_____	_____
14. post + test	_____	_____
15. in + accurate	_____	_____
16. dis + qualify	_____	_____

C Write three sentences. Use one of the words you created in Section B in each.

1. _____

_____

_____

2. _____

_____

_____

3. _____

_____

_____

Name _____

Supporting Details

⭐ In a unified paragraph, all the sentences work together to develop one main idea. You can develop the main idea with related facts, statistics, reasons, or examples.

In the paragraph below, the writer supports the topic sentence with three facts. Notice that the topic sentence is not the first sentence in the paragraph. Also notice how the underlined words and phrases relate the supporting facts to the main idea.

> Water is essential to the survival of the Everglades. Water used to flow freely into the Everglades from Lake Okeechobee. <u>Today, less water is reaching the Everglades because of development in the surrounding region.</u> Where is the water going? <u>Some of it</u> is being used by large farms to irrigate fields. <u>Much of it</u> is held in ponds to drain large areas of land so that houses and businesses can be built. The water <u>also</u> supplies the needs of people in the newly developed areas.

 Read the paragraph, which expresses an opinion. In the outline below, identify the main idea, two reasons that support the main idea, and two facts that support each reason. State the reasons and facts in your own words.

We need to do everything we can to save the Everglades. This wetland in southern Florida has a unique environment. Both tropical and cool-weather plants and animals live in this diverse ecosystem. There are hundreds of types of plants and over 300 kinds of birds, including many wading birds, such as the ibis. Mammals such as the manatee and the Florida panther also live there. Today, this fragile ecosystem is threatened, as shown by the shrinking number of animals. For example, there are only about 10 percent of the number of ibises that existed in the 1930s. In addition, the manatee, the crocodile, and the Florida panther have become endangered species.

Topic sentence (opinion): _____

   A. First reason: _____

      1. Supporting fact: _____

      2. Supporting fact: _____

   B. Second reason: _____

      1. Supporting fact: _____

      2. Supporting fact: _____

B **Write a paragraph for the topic sentence using the facts listed below. Reword the facts as needed to relate them to the topic sentence or each other.**

Kilauea, which lies partly within Hawaii Volcanoes National Park, is a young volcano that is still active. _____

_____

_____ first sentence _____

_____

_____

_____

_____

_____

_____

_____

_____

_____

_____

_____

_____

_____

_____

_____

_____

_____

_____

Supporting facts:
- The volcano's name means "much spewing."
- Kilauea has erupted more than fifty times since 1980.
- In the 1980s, repeated and violent eruptions caused much damage along the park's eastern border.
- In 1989, a flow of molten rock swept away a visitors center at the park.
- After these eruptions, a new cone rose over 700 feet tall.

Name _____

Editing Your Work

 Editing your work is an important step in the writing process. Many tests ask you to show what you know about editing.

A **Kareem wrote an account of his trip to Mammoth Cave. Help him revise and edit his work. Read the first two paragraphs below, and then answer the questions.**

1) Mammoth Cave is a fascinating park because it is all under ground. 2) More than 350 miles of caves make it the world's longest known cave system. 3) Rangers lead tours on the ten miles of passages that are open to the public. 4) On these hikes, you are 200 or 300 feet below the surface of the earth. 5) You pass through narrow passageways and huge open rooms. 6) You see many beautiful rock formations, including stalactites, which look like icicles.

7) We got to the visitors center at 8;00 a.m. 8) There we found out that the temperature under ground is always in the mid-50s to the low 60s. 9) We were glad we will have brought our jackets.

1. Are the supporting details in the first paragraph reasons or facts?

_____

2. In sentence 3, what subordinate clause describes the word *passages*? Is this sentence punctuated correctly?

_____

3. Sentence 7 contains a punctuation error. Write the sentence correctly.

_____

4. What types of sentences are used in paragraph 2?

_____

5. Rewrite sentence 9 to correct the error.

_____

Advantage Grammar Grade 7 © 2005 Creative Teaching Press

Name _____

B Continue reading Kareem's account of his trip. Help him revise his work by answering the questions below.

1) There were three tours to chose from; the Historic Tour, the Grand Avenue Tour, and the Introduction to Caving Tour. 2) My family and I chose the Historic Tour. 3) On this trip which is two hours long you go in through an entrance that the Native Americans had used for thousands of years. 4) A brochure gave us a preview of the tour.

5) The route was lighted, although the light was not bright. 6) As I walked along, one question stayed in my mind, How dark would it be without any light at all. 7) When we got to Mammoth Dome, a huge room that is 192 feet high, I had a chance to find out. 8) The ranger gathered everyone around him. 9) After a warning, he switched off the lights. 10) Ooooh. 11) The startled crowd seemed to make one sound. 12) Quickly the ranger lit a match, and I saw a tiny circle of faces around it. 13) By the time we got back to daylight, the sky will have clouded over, but it was still hard to adjust to the brightness.

1. What change in punctuation should be made in sentence 1?

   _____

2. In sentence 3, what nonessential clause should be set off with commas?

   _____

3. Which word in sentence 4 has a prefix? What does the prefix mean?

   _____

4. In sentence 6 there are two punctuation errors. Write the sentence correctly.

   _____

5. What correction should be made in sentence 10? Why?

   _____

6. Rewrite sentence 13 to correct an error in the use of the perfect tense.

   _____

   _____

Name _____

Fill in the bubble beside the correct answer.

Yong prepared an announcement for everyone going on the trip to the Great Smokey Mountains National Park. Help him revise and edit the announcement.

1) Attention Fellow Travelers:

2) We are looking forward to our class camping trip to the Great Smokies. 3) Everyone who has signed up for the trip should follow these tips and instructions:

- 4) The van will leave the town square at 7:30 a.m. 5) Please arrive at least 30 minutes early to help with loading.
- 6) Each person should bring the following items sleeping bag, pad, pillow, knapsack, water bottle, boots, and clothing for both wet and dry weather. 7) It is unnecessary to bring tents since we will be camping in a wood shelter.
- 8) It's summertime. 9) Don't forget to bring tick and mosquito repellant.
- 10) A midmorning snack will be provided in the van.

11) As a special treat, Mr. Teasdale has agreed to bring his guitar. 12) (By the time we get to the Smokies, I bet we had sung fifty songs!)

1. Which of the following is an imperative sentence?

   Ⓐ sentence 2   Ⓒ sentence 4

   Ⓑ sentence 3   Ⓓ sentence 5

2. In sentence 6, where is a colon needed?

   Ⓕ after *person*   Ⓗ after *boots*

   Ⓖ after *items*   Ⓙ after *clothing*

3. What do the words *unnecessary* (in sentence 7) and *midmorning* (in sentence 10) have in common?

   Ⓐ Both are nouns.   Ⓒ Both are incorrectly spelled.

   Ⓑ Both have prefixes.   Ⓓ Both are in the perfect tense.

4. What change should be made in sentence 12?

   Ⓕ Change the comma to a colon.

   Ⓖ Change the period to a question mark.

   Ⓗ Add commas around *had sung*.

   Ⓙ Change *had sung* to *will have sung*.

During his trip in the Smokies, Yong wrote a postcard to his grandfather. Help him revise and edit what he wrote.

1) Dear Grandad:

2) I've always wanted to go to the Smokies, and now I'm finally here. 3) Today we walked part of the Appalachian Trail. 4) Did you know the trail goes all the way from Georgia to Maine? 5) Along the way, I saw many examples of the neat wildlife here. 6) The first creature I saw was a slimy salamander near the edge of a creek. 7) White-tailed deer can be seen nearly every day, at dawn or dusk, when they come out into open areas. 8) Yesterday, I saw a raccoon napping on the branch of a yellow poplar tree. 9) This morning we even saw a black bear dining on wild berries. 10) Luckily, he was far away! 11) The park ranger, who happens to be from our town, pointed out the bear to our group.

Love,
Yong

5. Which punctuation error should be corrected?
Ⓐ Change the colon after *Grandad* to a comma.
Ⓑ Change the period in sentence 2 to a question mark.
Ⓒ Change the period in sentence 3 to an exclamation mark.
Ⓓ Change the question mark in sentence 4 to a period.

6. In Yong's paragraph, how is the main idea supported?
Ⓕ by reasons
Ⓖ by facts
Ⓗ by statistics
Ⓙ by examples

7. What type of sentence is sentence 4?
Ⓐ a statement
Ⓑ an exclamation
Ⓒ a question
Ⓓ a command

8. Which statement is true about sentence 11?
Ⓕ It contains a nonessential subordinate clause.
Ⓖ It contains an essential subordinate clause.
Ⓗ It contains a nonessential independent clause.
Ⓙ It contains a verb in the past-perfect tense.

Name _____

Infinitives

25

THE INCREDIBLE
HUMAN BODY

⭐ An **infinitive** is a form of verb that is preceded by the word *to*. It can serve as a noun, adjective, or adverb in a sentence.

  To eat is usually a pleasure. (noun)
  Here is a carrot *to eat*. (adjective)
  At six we are going *to eat*. (adverb)

Infinitives often occur in phrases. An infinitive phrase includes the infinitive plus any words that modify it.

  To loose five pounds is Tom's goal. (noun phrase as subject)
  Tom wants *to loose five pounds*. (noun phrase as direct object)
  Here is a carrot *to eat later as a snack*. (adjective phrase)
  We are planning *to have lunch in the cafeteria*. (adverb phrase)

Ⓐ **Underline the infinitive phrase in each sentence. Circle the infinitive. If there is no infinitive, draw a line through the sentence.**

1. The digestive system has an important job to do.

2. Digestion begins when you start to chew your food.

3. The teeth crush and cut the food so it is easier to swallow.

4. Saliva in the mouth starts to digest starches in the food.

5. Then the tongue moves the food to the back of the throat.

6. Swallowing causes the food to move into the esophagus.

7. The esophagus is a tube that leads to the stomach.

8. The stomach can stretch to fill up with food.

9. Stomach juices help to break down proteins in the food.

10. Stomach muscles contract to mix the food with its highly acidic juices.

 Advantage Grammar Grade 7 © 2005 Creative Teaching Press

B Complete each sentence with an infinitive phrase using a form of the verb in parentheses. Write about food or nutrition.

1. (eat) Robert does not like _____ .

2. (cook) _____ is not difficult.

3. (explain) This diagram helps _____ .

4. (read) Remember _____ .

5. (find out) You can use food labels _____ .

6. (lose) Shaun is hoping _____ .

7. (have) People need _____ for good health.

8. (chew) You can aid digestion by remembering _____ .

9. (serve) At the picnic, the parents are planning _____ .

10. (consume) One of my nutrition goals is _____ .

C Write a short paragraph about a food that you enjoy. Use two or three infinitives in your paragraph.

_____

_____

_____

_____

_____

_____

_____

_____

_____

_____

Participles

26

THE INCREDIBLE
HUMAN BODY

★ A **participle** is a verb form that serves as a modifier. The present participle always ends in *-ing*. The past participle ends in *-ed*, unless the verb is irregular. These endings turn an action word into an adjective.

Present participle:	Maya used a *drinking* cup. (drink)
	That soup has a *pleasing* smell. (please)
Past participle:	A *watched* pot never boils. (watch)
	Sam revealed the *hidden* pie. (hide, irregular)

A participle may occur in a phrase, which has an object. The entire participial phrase acts as an adjective in the sentence.

The man **cooking the soup** is my uncle.

Stirring the soup, my uncle smiled at me.

Estella carried a bowl **filled with apples**.

Filled with apples, the bowl was heavy.

A **State whether the underlined word is a present or past participle. Then write a sentence of your own using the participle.**

1. <u>spilled</u> milk _____

_____

2. <u>eating</u> habits _____

_____

3. <u>digested</u> food _____

_____

4. <u>burnt</u> toast _____

_____

5. <u>swallowing</u> process _____

_____

6. <u>boiling</u> water _____

_____

7. <u>completed</u> on time _____

_____

     Advantage Grammar Grade 7 © 2005 Creative Teaching Press

B Draw a line from the underlined participle to the noun it modifies.

1. The partly <u>digested</u> food passes from the stomach to the small intestine.

2. The small intestine is a long and complexly <u>folded</u> tube.

3. The food follows a <u>twisting</u> and <u>turning</u> path through this organ.

4. Chemicals <u>secreted</u> in the middle section of the intestine further break down the food.

5. Tiny fingerlike nubs <u>lining</u> the lower intestine absorb molecules of nutrients.

C Complete each sentence with the present or past participle form of the verb in parentheses. Then underline the participial phrase.

1. The nubs, _____ villi, contain many blood vessels.
   (call)

2. Nutrients _____ into the bloodstream are used by the body.   (absorb)

3. _____ in the blood, the nutrients go first to the liver.
   (travel)

4. Releasing some nutrients and _____ others until needed, the liver performs many different jobs.   (store)

D Rewrite each sentence to correct the form of the participle.

1. All food comes from lived things.

   _____

2. A varying diet will help you to stay healthy.

   _____

3. A balancing diet contains the right amounts of proteins, carbohydrates, fats, minerals, and vitamins.

   _____

Name _____

Using the Active and Passive Voices

★ **Voice** refers to whether the subject of the verb acts or is acted upon. A sentence is in the **active voice** when the subject of the verb performs the action. It is in the **passive voice** when the subject of the verb receives the action.

Active	**Passive**
Meg *won* the race.	The race *was won* by Meg.
The lungs *take in* air.	Air is *taken in* by the lungs.

Using the active voice adds strength and liveliness to your writing. Use the passive voice only when you have a good reason for doing so.

As the chest expands, air is drawn into the lungs through the nose.

In this example, using passive voice calls attention to where the air is going. Passive voice tends to be more useful and common in scientific and technical writing.

A **Read each sentence. On the line, note whether it is written in active voice (A) or passive voice (P).**

_____ **1.** Your body needs oxygen, an essential element.

_____ **2.** The lungs extract oxygen from the air.

_____ **3.** Inside the lungs, oxygen passes into the blood through the walls of branching airways.

_____ **4.** Red blood cells collect the oxygen and distribute it throughout the body.

_____ **5.** Oxygen is used by cells to create energy from the food you eat.

_____ **6.** The process of breathing in air, removing oxygen from it, and using it to convert food into energy is called respiration.

_____ **7.** After taking its first breath, the newborn baby cried.

_____ **8.** With the air we breathe in, we laugh, scream, talk, and sing.

_____ **9.** A trained opera singer uses her lungs to the fullest.

_____ **10.** The lungs are protected by the rib cage.

     Advantage Grammar Grade 7 © 2005 Creative Teaching Press

B **Read each sentence. If it is in the passive voice, rewrite it in active voice. If it is in active voice, change it to passive voice.**

1. My food was eaten too quickly, so I got the hiccups.

   _____

2. Sometimes the hiccups can be cured by holding your breath.

   _____

3. The race was won by the fastest sprinter.

   _____

4. With each breath, about two cupfuls of air are inhaled and exhaled by you.

   _____

   _____

5. When you sneeze, you expel air from your nose at 99 miles per hour!

   _____

   _____

C **Rewrite the paragraph to make it clearer and livelier.**

1. The singer on the stage took a deep breath. A long musical phrase could be sung by her with this air. The concert hall was filled by the sound of her voice. The singer was applauded enthusiastically by the audience.

   _____

   _____

   _____

   _____

   _____

   _____

   _____

   _____

   _____

   _____

Using Hyphens and Dashes

28

THE INCREDIBLE HUMAN BODY

⭐ The **hyphen** (-) is a mark of separation used between the parts of a word. Many compound words are spelled with hyphens. Generally, words in the following categories take hyphens:

Type of Word	Example
Self, ex, or *all,* plus another word	self-control, ex-player, all-knowing
Numerals from *twenty-one* to *ninety-nine*	forty-seven, sixty-six, eighty-nine
Fractions used as modifiers	two-fifths full, one-half ton
Adjective or adverb* plus participle	much-loved story, sweet-smelling rose

(*Exception: Do not use a hyphen between an *-ly* adverb and a participle, as in *completely finished report.*)

Many compound nouns and adjectives are spelled with hyphens.

Adjectives: able-bodied soldier, two-year-old girl, seventh-grade student

Nouns: know-it-all, great-grandfather, tattle-tale

However, some compounds (such as *high school*) are spelled "open," while many others (such as *footprint*) are spelled "closed up." Refer to a dictionary if you are unsure of how to spell a compound word.

The **dash** (—) is used to show a sudden break or change in thought. A dash often signals an element of surprise or emotion.

I think—no, I'm certain—that blood is thicker than water.

If there is no break or change in thought, use commas.

I know, because I just read it, that blood is thicker than water.

A dash can also be used to give emphasis to an idea or thought within the sentence.

It's a wonderful present—just the one I wanted.

A Read each sentence. Add hyphens to the words that need them.

1. The volleyball team is wearing green warm up suits.

2. Enrico is a hard playing member of the Bobcats.

3. He is a soft spoken young man who is highly respected by his teammates.

4. All the members of the team have plenty of self confidence.

5. The captain is the ex president of the computer club.

6. Last Friday night we watched a game with a hair raising ending.

B Rewrite each sentence, adding dashes where they are needed.

1. On Saturday or perhaps it was Sunday we went to the track meet.

   _____

2. If you see Dwayne wait a minute, there he is now tell him we'll be at the gate.

   _____

   _____

3. It was an amazing race a race that I will never forget.

   _____

4. Jerry I don't know if he can win or not just completed the first lap of the race.

   _____

   _____

5. His finishing time this is incredible was three minutes and fifteen seconds!

   _____

C Write a phrase that fits each clue. Include a compound adjective that is hyphenated.

Example: a flower that smells sweet   <u>sweet-smelling flower</u>

1. a sword with an edge like a knife _____

2. a kite that can fly high _____

3. a story with just one side _____

4. a family that has enough money _____

D Match the clue with the correct hyphenated noun. Write the letter of the correct noun on the line.

_____ 1. guy who is always there when needed

_____ 2. someone with lots of different skills

_____ 3. person who is no longer a soldier

_____ 4. someone who spoils the fun

a. ex-soldier
b. Johnny-on-the-spot
c. jack-of-all-trades
d. stick-in-the-mud

LESSON

29

THE INCREDIBLE
HUMAN BODY

Suffixes

★ Knowing how to add suffixes to words can help you avoid spelling errors. A suffix is a letter or group of letters added to the end of a word to change its use and meaning.

Suffix	Changes . . .	Example
-ly	an adjective to an adverb	kind→kindly (in a kind manner)
-ness	an adjective to a noun	even→evenness (quality of being even)
-y	a noun to an adjective	dirt→dirty (having the quality of dirt)

The spelling of most words does not change when you add the suffix *-ly*, *-ness*, or *-y*. Exceptions are summarized in the chart.

Suffix	If the word ends in . . .	Then . . .	Example
-ly	A single *l*	Keep the *l*.	special + ly = specially
	A double *l*	Drop one *l*.	full + ly = fully
	A consonant + *le*	Drop the *le*.	terrible + ly = terribly
-ness	A *y* after a consonant	Change the *y* to *i*.	stick + y = stickiness
-y	Silent *e*	Drop the *e*.	ice + y = icy
	A consonant after a single vowel	Double the consonant.	spot + y = spotty
	A consonant after two vowels	Do not double the consonant.	seed + y = seedy

A Change each adjective to an adverb by adding *-ly*. Write the adverb on the line.

1. playful _____
2. cool _____
3. typical _____
4. terrible _____
5. able _____
6. open _____
7. efficient _____
8. body _____

9. careful _____
10. strong _____
11. rapid _____
12. dull _____
13. forceful _____
14. complete _____
15. double _____
16. busy _____

 Advantage Grammar Grade 7 © 2005 Creative Teaching Press

B Complete the second sentence in each pair by changing the underlined adjective to a noun. Add *-ness* to create the noun.

1. One of the basketball players was very <u>thin</u>.

   Many people noticed his _____ .

2. The tennis player's injured knee was <u>painful</u>.

   The _____ of her injury kept her from playing.

3. The <u>sudden</u> impact of the ball startled her.

   The _____ of the impact startled her.

4. In spite of losing the game, the team was <u>happy</u> with their performance.

   Their _____ was evident in the smiles on their faces.

5. The <u>open</u> field was a good place to play soccer.

   The _____ of the field allowed us to play soccer.

6. The <u>heavy</u> weights were hard to lift.

   The _____ of the weights made them hard to lift.

7. By the end of the game, both players were <u>short</u> of breath.

   Both players experienced a _____ of breath at the end of the game.

8. In the stands, a <u>large</u> crowd cheered the athletes on.

   The fine weather accounted for the _____ of the crowd.

C Circle the correctly spelled word in parentheses to complete each sentence.

1. A doctor will decide if the operation is (medicaly, medically) necessary.

2. After running in the 400-meter race, Todd was very (sweatty, sweaty)

3. Anyone who completes a marathon will be (totaly, totally) exhausted.

4. They (fuly, fully) understand the need for daily exercise.

5. Although the conditions were (icy, icey), Willie went skiing anyway.

6. Danton is (possibly, possibley) the best runner on the team.

7. That wrestler is known for the (trickiness, trickyness) of his moves.

8. Ichiko (agreeably, agreeabley) threw the ball to the young children.

Name _____

Transitional Words and Phrases

⭐ **Transitional words** are the links and bridges between related statements
or ideas in a paragraph. These links make it easier for the reader to
follow the flow of thought from sentence to sentence. Transitional words
are usually placed at the beginning of a sentence.

The choice of transitional words often depends on the type of organization
used in the paragraph.

Type of Organization	Transitional Words
Chronological	first, second, next, in the past, today
Spatial	next to, above, below, beyond
Compare and contrast	likewise, similarly, compared to, on the other hand
Cause and effect	as a result, therefore, one cause of, another effect of
Order of importance	most important, less important

Many other words and phrases can be used to show the relationship between
statements and ideas. Here are just a few:

for example	evidently	actually	overall
since then	in fact	generally	also

 A **Read each group of sentences. Look for words that help to show the
relationship between pieces of information or ideas. Write these transitional
words and phrases on the line.**

1. The lungs are an important part of the respiratory system. They have two main
jobs to do. First, they get oxygen from the air into the bloodstream. Second,
they remove waste gas, or carbon dioxide.

_____

2. The lungs are filled with many blood vessels. As a result, they have a pinkish
red color. They also contain a branching system of air-filled tubes, so they feel
spongy.

_____

3. Each lung is divided into parts called lobes. The right lung has three lobes. The
left lung, on the other hand, has two to allow room for the heart.

_____

Name _____

B **Write the phrase that best completes each sentence.**

> For example,   In fact,   Also,   The most important

1. There are many reasons to run. _____ one is that it is good for your heart.
2. Running improves circulation. _____ it can help you lose weight.
3. Runners need carbohydrates. _____ they might eat spaghetti the night before a race.
4. Nikki's heart rate was in the normal range. _____ it was 72 beats per minute.

C **Add appropriate transition words from the list to each paragraph. On the line before the paragraph, note whether the paragraph uses chronological (C), spatial (S), or cause-and-effect (CE) organization.**

> below   first   then   another result
> left   right   therefore   finally

_____ 1. Zachary decided to use the step machine at the fitness center. _____ he read the instructions on the control panel. _____ he punched in his weight and height. _____ he selected the level of difficulty from the three choices: city stroll, cross-country, or Mount Everest!

_____ 2. Asthma is a breathing problem. It occurs when smooth muscle fibers around the bronchioles (the smallest tubes in the lungs) contract. This causes the airways to narrow. _____ the person feels out of breath. _____ is wheezing or coughing episodes.

_____ 3. Nat's science fair project is on the respiratory system. _____ the title, "Breathe Easy," is a diagram of the lungs. On the _____ panel are color photographs of a healthy lung and a cancerous lung. On the _____ panel is a graph that compares the lung capacities of a marathon runner and an average person.

Name _____

 Editing your work is an important step in the writing process. Many tests ask you to show what you know about editing.

A Read Greg's account of visiting a bloodmobile. Then answer the questions to help him revise and edit his work.

Giving Blood

1) It's easy to take the blood in your body for granted—until you need some. 2) Blood is often needed when people are operated on in hospitals. 3) Also, people in car accidents often lose blood and must have it replaced.

4) This replacement blood comes from donors, everyday people who volunteer to give a pint of blood. 5) Blood can be donated at a clinic or any bloodmobile. 6) Recently, I visited a bloodmobile with my dad—who had decided to donate blood. 7) I saw six people waiting calmly for their turn. 8) I admired their self sacrifice.

1. What is the function of the dash in sentence 1?

_____

2. Which sentence in the first paragraph is written in passive voice?

_____

3. In sentence 4, identify the infinitive phrase.

_____

4. Rewrite sentence 5 in the active voice.

_____

_____

5. Rewrite sentence 6 to correct the punctuation error.

_____

_____

6. Sentence 8 contains a spelling error. Write the word correctly.

_____

Name _____

B **Continue reading Greg's report. Answer the questions to help him edit and revise his report.**

   1) The donors seemed to fully understand what would happen. 2) Each one was asked to lie down on a hospital bed. 3) Then a medical technician inserted a needle into a vein in the person's arm. 4) The needle was connected by tubes to a small, sturdy plastic bag hanging on a nearby stand. 5) When the bag was about two thirds full, I asked my dad how he felt. 6) He said he felt fine. 7) Sometimes the loss of blood makes a donor feel light headed. 8) However, the body soon replaces the lost blood.
   9) To give blood is easy. 10) It doesn't take long, and it is not painful. 11) Most importantly, giving blood helps save lives.

1. In sentence 1, is the word *fully* spelled correctly? What is the base word and suffix in this word?

   _____

2. In sentence 4, what verb form is the word *hanging*? What word does it modify?

   _____

3. Find two compound adjectives that need hyphens. Correctly spell the words below.

   _____

4. What is the function of the transitional word in sentence 8?

   _____

5. Is the word *lost* in sentence 8 a past or present participle? How does it function as a part of speech in this sentence?

   _____

6. Identify the infinitive phrase in sentence 9.

   _____

Name _____

32

THE INCREDIBLE
HUMAN BODY

Take a Test Drive

Fill in the bubble beside the correct answer.

Diana wrote an essay about the circulatory system. Help her revise and edit her work. Read Diana's essay and follow the directions.

The Heart and More

1) The cardiovascular system includes the heart, the blood, and a network of blood vessels throughout the body. 2) This system has several important functions. 3) It is a delivery system. 4) For example, it delivers oxygen from the lungs and nutrients from the digestive system to all parts of the body. 5) Waste products are also moved from the body's cells to places where they can leave the body.

6) A second function of this system is protection. 7) White blood cells in the blood defend the body against infection. 8) In addition, the cardiovascular system prevents blood loss through clotting. 9) The third function of the circulatory system is regulation. 10) For example, it helps to keep the body at a constant temperature by distributing heat.

1. What transition should be added at the beginning of sentence 3?
- Ⓐ As a result,
- Ⓒ Then,
- Ⓑ First of all,
- Ⓓ Actually,

2. How should sentence 5 be changed?
- Ⓕ Change it from passive voice to active voice.
- Ⓖ Add a dash after the word *places*.
- Ⓗ Change the word *moved* to *moving*.
- Ⓙ It should not be changed at all.

3. Which statement is true about the second paragraph?
- Ⓐ It uses many words with hyphens.
- Ⓒ It uses spatial organization.
- Ⓑ It uses transitions effectively.
- Ⓓ It is written in passive voice.

4. In sentence 10, what is the complete infinitive phrase?
- Ⓕ to keep
- Ⓖ to keep the body
- Ⓗ to keep the body at a constant temperature
- Ⓙ to keep the body at a constant temperature by distributing heat

     Advantage Grammar Grade 7 © 2005 Creative Teaching Press

Name _____

Continue reading and editing Diana's essay.

1) Blood—in my opinion, the most interesting part of the system is a tissue. 2) It is made up of red and white bloods cells that float in a liquid called plasma. 3) Red blood cells carry much-needed oxygen to other tissues in the body. 4) White blood cells destroy disease-causing microorganisms.

5) Special cells called platelets are also part of the blood. 6) Their role is to stop bleeding. 7) Platelets are about one-third the size of red blood cells. 8) When a blood vessel is cut, the plates become swollen, spikie, and sticky. 9) The stickyness of the platelets makes them stay at the site of damage. 10) The swollen platelets attract other platelets. 11) They join together to form a temporary plug that stops blood loss.

5. How should sentence 1 be changed?
- Ⓐ Add a dash after the word *part*.
- Ⓑ Add a dash after the word *system*.
- Ⓒ Add a hyphen after the word *most*.
- Ⓓ Add a hyphen after the word *system*.

6. Which label fits the word *much-needed* in sentence 3?
- Ⓕ past participle
- Ⓖ present participle
- Ⓗ active verb
- Ⓙ past-tense verb

7. In sentence 4, what word does *disease-causing* modify?
- Ⓐ blood
- Ⓑ cells
- Ⓒ destroy
- Ⓓ microorganisms

8. What two words in sentences 8 and 9 are misspelled?
- Ⓕ *spikie* and *sticky*
- Ⓖ *spikie* and *stickyness*
- Ⓗ *swollen* and *sticky*
- Ⓙ *swollen* and *stay*

Name _____

33

LITERATURE

Gerunds

⭐ Gerunds, like participles and infinitives, are verb forms. Gerunds function as nouns in a sentence and always end in *-ing*.
   Fran's *writing* has improved.

A compound gerund has a noun before the gerund.
   Mountain climbing is his hobby.

A gerund phrase has an object.
   Hans enjoys *reading to little children*.

Gerunds can look like participles because both end in *-ing*. To tell if the word is a gerund, study how it is used in the sentence. If it serves as a noun, then it is a gerund.
   Participles: Fran is *writing* a letter. (verb)
              The girl *writing* the letter is Fran. (adjective)
   Gerund: *Writing* letters is easy for her. (noun)

A Underline the gerund or gerund phrase in each sentence. If you do not find a gerund, draw a line through the sentence.

1. Research is the process of gathering ideas and information.
2. Libraries are one of the best places for finding information.
3. Locating books at the library is not difficult.
4. Libraries generally use one of two systems for classifying books.
5. Most school and public libraries have been using the Dewey Decimal System.
6. Becoming familiar with the Dewey Decimal System is a good idea.
7. When you want to locate a book, finding out the call number is the first step.
8. You can find the call number by typing in a search in the online catalog.
9. Once you find the record, writing down the call number is a good idea.
10. By using the signs at the ends of the bookshelves, you can find the shelf that contains the call numbers close to yours.
11. After the book signing, the library staff took the author out to lunch.
12. Brad looked at a display of books on diving.

B Participles are used as adjectives or verbs, whereas gerunds are always used as nouns. Read each pair of sentences. Place a check next to the sentence that contains a gerund or gerund phrase.

1. _____ Tanya returned the missing book.

   _____ Missing the bus made her late for school.

2. _____ You should give swimming a try.

   _____ The swimming coach showed me a book about famous Olympic athletes.

3. _____ The shelves containing those books are in the back.

   _____ Containing our excitement was impossible.

4. _____ She saw two students collecting books for the sale.

   _____ Will you help me with collecting the books?

5. _____ Nan found an article treating that topic in volume A of the encyclopedia.

   _____ My aunt is fond of treating us to ice cream.

6. _____ Try searching for that book with a keyword.

   _____ Connie is searching for an answer to her question.

C Complete each sentence with a gerund or gerund phrase. Use a form of the verb in parentheses. (*Tip:* When a word ends in a silent *e*, drop the *e* before adding *-ing*.)

1. Douglas discovered which city has the most people by _____ an almanac. (consult)

2. The quickest way to find a topic in a book is by _____ it up in the index. (look)

3. Robert enjoys _____ the fiction section at the library. (browse)

4. The key to _____ his attention is an unusual title. (catch)

5. _____ a thesaurus when you write is a good way to expand your vocabulary. (use)

6. _____ his vocabulary is one of Stan's goals. (improve)

34

LITERATURE

Pronouns and Antecedents

⭐ Readers can get confused when pronouns and antecedents don't agree. The antecedent is the word or group of words that a pronoun refers to. A pronoun must agree with its antecedent in gender (masculine, feminine, or neuter) and number (singular or plural).

The man put on **his** coat.　　She put on **her** coat.　　They put on **their** coats.

The antecedent often comes before the pronoun that stands for it, but not always.

Because the man wore a coat, **he** was not cold.

Because **he** was cold, the man put on a coat.

Indefinite pronouns refer to people, places, or things in a more general way. When choosing an indefinite pronoun, check to see if the antecedent is singular or plural.

Each put on **his** or **her** coat.　　　Several put on **their** coats.

Each of them put on **his** or **her** coat.　Several of them put on **their** coats.

Here are some examples of singular and plural indefinite pronouns.

Singular: each, no one, one, nobody, everybody, anyone, someone, another

Plural: all, some, both, many, plenty, several, more, most, few, others

---

 In each sentence or pair of sentences, circle the antecedent of the underlined pronoun.

1. Lawrence enjoys listening to poetry on <u>his</u> CD player.

2. This poem gets <u>its</u> impact from rhyme and repetition.

3. Eve Merriam and Nikki Giovanni read <u>their</u> poems from the stage.

4. Although Eve Merriam is best known for her poetry, <u>she</u> also writes plays and fiction.

5. The poem about the old barn appealed to the audience. <u>Some</u> had heard it before.

6. Because <u>they</u> arrived early, the three students were able to talk to the speaker.

　　　　　　　　　　　　　　　　　　Advantage Grammar Grade 7 © 2005 Creative Teaching Press

B Read each pair of sentences. Place a check next to the sentence in which the underlined pronoun agrees with its antecedent.

1. _____ All of the students said <u>they</u> would help.

   _____ Each of the girls said <u>they</u> would help.

2. _____ Nobody remembered to bring <u>their</u> notebook.

   _____ Nobody remembered to bring <u>his or her</u> notebook.

3. _____ Many in the audience said that poetry gives <u>them</u> comfort.

   _____ Many in the audience said that poetry gives <u>him</u> comfort.

4. _____ Every one of the girls was giving the speaker <u>her</u> complete attention.

   _____ Every one of the girls was giving the speaker <u>their</u> complete attention.

5. _____ Everybody liked the poem, but three or four said <u>they</u> loved it.

   _____ Everybody liked the poem, but three or four said <u>she</u> loved it.

C Rewrite the sentence or sentences to make the pronoun agree with its antecedent.

1. Someone left their notebook on one of the seats at the poetry reading.

   _____

2. Each of the poems has her own theme.

   _____

3. The three poets were at the bookstore. All had agreed to sign his books.

   _____

4. Cassandra gave his most expressive reading yet of Frost's poem "Birches."

   _____

5. Make sure that each reader has somebody to listen to them.

   _____

Name _____

 Some sentences have a main clause and a subordinate clause. The **main clause** states the most important idea in the sentence and can stand by itself. The **subordinate clause** is less important and cannot stand alone. It depends on the main clause to complete its meaning.

When we looked at the feeder, we saw the hummingbird.
(subordinate clause)   (main clause)

In this sentence, the subordinate clause is used as an adverb. It describes the verb *saw*. Adverb clauses add information about the time, place, manner, condition, or cause of the action stated in the verb. Adverb clauses are introduced by subordinate conjunctions such as the following:

when, before, while, since, until (time)
where, wherever (place)
as, as if (manner)
if, so, unless, in order that, although (condition)
because, since, as a result of (cause)

An adverbial clause at the beginning of a sentence is usually followed by a comma. When the main clause comes first, a comma is generally not used unless the adverbial clause contains nonessential information.

We saw the hummingbird when we looked at the feeder.
We saw the hummingbird, although it was gone in a flash.

A **Underline the subordinate clause in each sentence.**

1. I enjoy Diane Ackerman's essays because they are about the natural world.

2. After I read "Mute Dancers: How to Watch a Hummingbird," I was hooked.

3. If you want to learn some fascinating facts about hummingbirds, read this essay.

4. Hummingbirds are fun to watch as they speed or dart from flower to flower.

5. When a hummingbird drinks nectar, it licks rapidly with its W-shaped tongue.

6. Because this tiny bird's heart beats 500 times a minute, it needs a lot of energy.

7. When the day ends, the little hummingbird is exhausted.

8. At night while the hummingbird is resting, its heart slows to just 36 beats a minute.

B Read each sentence. If a comma is needed, add it to the sentence. If the sentence is correct, write *C* on the line.

_____ **1.** A hummingbird in flight makes a constant soft drone, as if it were a bee.

_____ **2.** As soon as a hummingbird lands the humming stops.

_____ **3.** This occurs because the humming sound comes from the bird's beating wings.

_____ **4.** Although hummingbirds "hum," they do not sing.

_____ **5.** Because they have only small voices they do not communicate like other birds.

_____ **6.** Whereas other birds sing out to find a mate or claim territory, hummingbirds do a dance.

_____ **7.** When they need to spell out a mood or a message they use body language, just as bees do.

_____ **8.** If you wear a red shirt a hummingbird may zoom up to you to see if you are a flower.

C Combine the two independent clauses using the subordinate conjunction in parentheses. Add a comma to set off the clause if needed.

1. We were delighted. We saw six hummingbirds at the feeder at one time. (when)

_____

_____

2. There are more kinds of hummingbirds near the equator. There are more flowers in warm climates. (because)

_____

_____

3. We could see hummingbirds. We looked in Mrs. Holman's garden. (wherever)

_____

_____

4. There are 16 species of hummingbirds in North America. There are dozens of species in South America. (although)

_____

_____

Name _____

36

LITERATURE

Using Quotation Marks

★ When you repeat, or copy, another person's words in your writing, you are using a direct quotation. Always enclose the other person's words in quotation marks. If the quotation is interrupted, enclose each part of the quotation with these marks.

> American writer William James said, "Wherever you are it is your own friends who make your world."
>
> "Wherever you are," William James said, "it is your own friends who make your world."

When quoting others, remember to do the following:

- Use a comma to separate quoted words from the rest of the sentence.
- Begin a direct quotation with a capital letter.
- Keep punctuation marks that belong to the direct quotation inside the quotation marks.

Quotation marks are also used to enclose the titles of short works.

> "The Open Window" (short story)
> "I to My Perils" (poem)
> "Mute Dancers" (article or essay)
> "Swing Low, Sweet Chariot" (song)

Titles of longer works such as books, magazines, newspapers, movies, and plays are italicized (or, in handwriting, underlined).

A **Rewrite each sentence, adding quotation marks and commas as needed.**

1. A Tibetan proverb states The goal will not be reached if the right distance is not traveled. _____

_____

2. In spite of everything, Anne Frank wrote in her diary I still believe that people are really good at heart. _____

_____

3. Reading is to the mind what exercise is to the body, wrote the eighteenth-century British author Richard Steele. _____

_____

    Advantage Grammar Grade 7 © 2005 Creative Teaching Press

B Read each sentence. Add quotation marks or underline each title that is mentioned.

1. For the poetry reading, Stan is planning to read How to Eat a Poem by Eve Merriam.

2. After reading the newspaper, she clipped the article How to Chop an Onion in Four Easy Steps.

3. Last weekend, we watched the movie Star Wars plus all of the sequels.

4. By the Light of the Silvery Moon is a very old-fashioned song that is often played on ukulele.

5. At the library, I chose The Moon by Whale Light, a nonfiction book by Diane Ackerman.

6. The Last Leaf is a typical O. Henry short story because it has a surprise ending.

7. I'll Fly Away is a folk song about escaping from prison, slavery, or some other unhappy situation.

8. Zeb likes to read the sports pages in USA Today, a very popular newspaper.

9. The Diary of Anne Frank was first performed at the Cort Theater in New York City in 1955.

10. The Tell-Tale Heart is one of Edgar Allan Poe's most famous and most chilling short stories.

C Skim a book, newspaper, or magazine to find interesting statements by several individuals. On the lines below, write out three direct quotations from your source. Be sure to identify the speaker in each case.

1. _____

_____

2. _____

_____

3. _____

_____

Name _____

 Certain words in English are often misspelled. Some of these are listed below. Knowing how to spell these words can help you avoid many errors.

absence	apparent	column	existence
abundant	attendance	committee	finally
accessible	breathe	conscious	independent
accurate	business	efficiency	influential
acquaintance	calendar	eighth	leisure
answer	clothes	embarrass	lightning

A Write the word from the list above that fits each clue. The first letter is provided.

1. Being away for a while   a __ __ __ __ __ __

2. Awake and aware   c __ __ __ __ __ __ __ __

3. After the seventh   e __ __ __ __ __

4. Not a question but an . . .   a __ __ __ __ __

5. Not a row but a . . .   c __ __ __ __ __

6. On your own   i __ __ __ __ __ __ __ __ __ __

B Complete each sentence with the correctly spelled word.

1. During his (lesure, leisure) time, Jason likes to read mysteries and play basketball.

2. Be sure to (breathe, breath) after each period when you read the poem.

3. Did you know that the author is an (aquaintence, acquaintance) of my uncle?

4. This short story is very (accessible, aksessible) because it describes everyday experiences.

5. This article is about gaining (efficiency, effishency) in doing your homework.

6. The (attendance, attendence) at the poetry reading was good.

C Complete each sentence with a word from the list.

accurate   business   clothes   lightning
committee   existence   finally   influential

1. After three weeks, I _____ finished *Watership Down*.

2. We read ghost stories by the fire as the _____ flashed outside the windows.

3. This author has been very _____ in advancing conservation laws.

4. Shauna was not aware of the _____ of a writers club at our school.

5. Several students formed a _____ to promote book reading.

6. The author wore casual _____ when he spoke to the class.

7. That newspaper journalist has written many articles about _____ and industry.

8. You can count on finding _____ statistics in her articles.

D Find each of the listed words in the puzzle. Circle the entire word. The words may be read from top to bottom, from left to right, or on a diagonal from left to right.

a	c	c	u	r	a	t	e	r	c
n	o	f	n	a	c	e	s	i	o
s	l	e	i	g	h	t	h	s	m
w	u	x	s	t	e	n	c	e	m
e	m	b	a	r	r	a	s	s	i
r	n	e	c	a	l	l	e	o	t
g	r	a	b	u	n	d	a	n	t
b	h	l	e	i	s	u	r	e	e
t	a	p	p	r	n	t	d	q	e
e	f	f	i	c	i	e	n	c	y

abundant   accurate

answer   breathe

column   committee

efficiency   eighth

embarrass   leisure

Name _____

Parallel Form

38

LITERATURE

 In writing, *parallel* means "similar" or "equal." A sentence has parallel form when you use the same grammatical form to express things or ideas of similar function or equal importance. Using **parallel form** will help make your writing correct, clear, and flowing.

> Faulty: Eve Merriam is a poet, fiction writer, and writes plays.
> Parallel: Eve Merriam is a **poet**, **fiction writer**, and **playwright**.

In the corrected sentence, notice that all three elements after the verb are expressed in the same way (as nouns) because they are equal in function and importance. Parallel form can be applied to words, phrases, clauses, and entire sentences.

> With words: For Betty, **reading** is more enjoyable than **writing**.
> With phrases: The sleigh went **over the river** and **through the woods**.
> With clauses: **When we laugh** and **when we cry**, we release our emotions.
> With sentences: **I long for the sun. I long for the sea. I long for the beach.**

A **Read each quotation. On the lines, write the words, phrases, or clauses that show parallel form.**

1. The inscription on the Statue of Liberty reads: "Give me your tired, your poor, your huddled masses yearning to breathe free."

   _____

2. In Abraham Lincoln's words, the American government is "of the people, by the people, and for the people."

   _____

3. "It was the best of times; it was the worst of times." (Charles Dickens)

   _____

4. "The sky is the only place where there is no prejudice. Up there, everyone is equal. Everyone is free." (Bessie Coleman)

   _____

5. "Champions aren't made in gyms. Champions are made from something they have deep inside them—a desire, a dream, a vision." (Muhammad Ali)

   _____

   _____

Advantage Grammar Grade 7 © 2005 Creative Teaching Press

B **Rewrite each sentence to correct the faulty parallelism.**

1. He described the rose as soft, delicate, and it smells sweet.

   _____

2. In his letter, he says he likes swimming, waterskiing, and to play chess.

   _____

3. World War II was fought on the land, on the sea, and using airplanes.

   _____

4. My goals are to do my best, to treat others kindly, and having a good time.

   _____

5. It's a bird! It's a plane! No, I see Superman!

   _____

C **Read the following paragraph about the seasons. Notice how the use of parallel form helps unify the paragraph and make it interesting to read. On the lines below, write your own paragraph about the seasons. Use parallel form at least twice in your paragraph.**

Every season has its joys. When spring arrives, birdsong is everywhere. The shoots of flowers nose their way through the warm earth. And my cat, Sarafina, catches her first mouse in the newly green grass. When summer comes, the yard turns shady, and crickets almost drown out the singing birds. And my cat, Sarafina, sprawls lazily in a sunny spot on the porch. When autumn comes, everything is orange and red. And Sarafina chases a twirling leaf. When winter comes, the trees are bare bones. The yard turns brown and the sky turns gray. And my cat, Sarafina, curls up snug in my lap.

_____

_____

_____

_____

_____

_____

39

LITERATURE

Editing Your Work

 Editing your work is an important step in the writing process. Many tests ask you to show what you know about editing.

 A **Neil wrote an essay about the folk hero Paul Bunyan. Help him edit and revise his work. Read the first few paragraphs, and then answer the questions that follow.**

1) In the essay Paul Bunyan of the North Woods, Carl Sandburg retells some of the popular stories about Paul Bunyan. 2) Carl Sandburg was very interested in American history and folklore. 3) He also wrote an influencial biography of Abraham Lincoln in 1940.

4) Paul Bunyan is a fictional character. 5) He is a giant of a man and very strong. 6) Paul is a lumberjack who lives in the woods near the Great Lakes. 7) He has a huge blue ox named Babe.

8) Long ago, people made up stories about Paul Bunyan to entertain each other. 9) In introducing Paul Bunyan, Sandburg writes Some of Paul is old as the hills, young as the alphabet. 10) People shared the stories by word of mouth. 11) Later on, as different writers wrote down the tales, they were shared in books.

1. Some punctuation is missing in sentence 1. Write the sentence correctly.

_____

_____

2. In sentence 3, how should the word before *biography* be spelled?

_____

3. Rewrite sentence 5 so that it uses parallel form.

_____

4. In sentence 9, where should quotation marks be inserted?

_____

5. Which sentence in the third paragraph uses parallel form? _____

6. Identify the adverbial clause in sentence 11.

_____

Advantage Grammar Grade 7 © 2005 Creative Teaching Press

B Continue reading Neil's essay. Help him edit and revise his work by answering the questions below.

1) Paul Bunyan stories are tall tales. 2) Exaggeration and humor are abundent in tall tales. 3) Here is an example from Sandburg's essay. 4) Paul was logging in Oregon one winter. 5) At the camp, there was a cookstove that covered a whole acre of ground. 6) To grease the griddle for pancakes, four men strapped big pieces of pork to his snowshoes and skated across the griddle. 7) Because the table for eating was three miles long, boys on bicycles rode back and forth down the center to serve the pancakes.

8) Here is another example of funny exaggeration. 9) One time, the Pacific Ocean froze over during the winter, and Paul harnessed teams of oxen to haul white snow over from China. 10) That same winter, Paul gave a party for his fellow lumberjacks. 11) He made a huge granite floor for them to dance on. 12) Their boots pounded the floor so hard that they caused an earthquake.

1. In sentence 2, how should the adjective after the word *are* be spelled?

_____

2. In sentence 6, what is the antecedent for the pronoun *his*? Rewrite the sentence to correct the error. _____

_____

_____

3. What is the gerund in sentence 7?

_____

4. What is similar about sentence 3 and sentence 8? How does this similarity help the reader? _____

_____

_____

_____

5. Which sentence in the first paragraph contains an adverbial clause?

_____

LESSON

40

LITERATURE

Take a Test Drive

Fill in the bubble beside the correct answer.

Lucy wrote a summary of an American folktale. Help her revise and edit her essay. Read the essay and answer the questions that follow.

Flying Away

1) "The People Could Fly" by Virginia Hamilton is a retelling of a folktale. 2) The tale takes place in the past, during the time when most African Americans lived as slaves on large plantations. 3) This American folktale is based on African folktales about magic and people who could fly like birds.

4) An old man named Toby and a young mother named Sarah, who carried her baby on her back, were working in the fields. 5) They worked under the watchful eye of the overseer and his driver. 6) He thought the slaves weren't working fast enough, so he cracked his whip. 7) When Sarah's baby cried, he yelled at her and cracked his whip some more. 8) Sarah's legs bled, and she fell to the ground.

1. Why did the writer use quotation marks around "The People Could Fly?"
   Ⓐ because Virginia Hamilton spoke these words
   Ⓑ because these words are the title of a book
   Ⓒ because these words are the title of a short story
   Ⓓ because these words are the title of a movie

2. Which sentence contains a gerund?
   Ⓕ sentence 1   Ⓗ sentence 6
   Ⓖ sentence 3   Ⓙ sentence 8

3. In sentence 6, what is the antecedent for the pronoun *He*?
   Ⓐ overseer   Ⓒ overseer and driver
   Ⓑ driver   Ⓓ The antecedent is unclear.

4. Which sentence contains an adverbial clause?
   Ⓕ sentence 5   Ⓗ sentence 7
   Ⓖ sentence 6   Ⓙ sentence 8

           Advantage Grammar Grade 7 © 2005 Creative Teaching Press

Name _____

Continue reading and editing Lucy's summary. Answer the questions below.

1) Toby came to her side. 2) Sarah pleaded, "Now, before it's too late." 3) Toby knew that the time had come. 4) He ansered, "Go, as you know how to go!" 5) Then he said the magic words, quickly and softly. 6) The young woman began to rise in the air. 7) Up and up she rose, free as a bird. 8) The overseer couldn't believe it, but there was nothing he could do.

9) The next day, the slaves' work was especially hard, because it was so hot. 10) When one slave after another collapsed from the heat, they felt the lash of over-seer's whip. 11) Toby spoke the ancient words over each one who had fallen. 12) Like Sarah, they rose into the air. 13) Like a flock of black crows, they flew away to freedom. 14) Those who could not fly were left behind. 15) But they remembered this vision of freedom, and they told their children about the people who could fly.

5. Which sentence in the first paragraph contains a commonly misspelled word?
Ⓐ sentence 3 Ⓒ sentence 5
Ⓑ sentence 4 Ⓓ sentence 6

6. In sentence 9, what correction should be made?
Ⓕ Change the period to a question mark.
Ⓖ Delete the comma after *hard*.
Ⓗ Change *hard* to *difficult*.
Ⓙ Delete *The next day*.

7. In sentence 10, the pronoun and antecedent do not agree. Which word is the best choice to replace the pronoun *they*?
Ⓐ you Ⓒ we
Ⓑ she Ⓓ each

8. In which two sentences did the writer use parallel form effectively?
Ⓕ sentences 4 and 5
Ⓖ sentences 7 and 8
Ⓗ sentences 10 and 11
Ⓙ sentences 12 and 13

Advantage Grammar Grade 7 © 2005 Creative Teaching Press

83

LESSON

41

JUST FOR FUN

Verb Agreement with Compound Subjects

★ A verb must agree with the subject in number. Two subjects joined by *and* require a plural verb.

>**Ben and Libby** *are* going to the county fair.

However, if the subject is thought of as one unit, the verb is singular.

>**Beans and rice** *is* my favorite dish.

If the subjects are joined by *or, either . . . or,* or *neither . . . nor,* the verb agrees with the subject that is closer to it.

>Ben or **Libby is** going to the fair.
>Ben or his **sisters are** going to meet you at the gate.
>Either they or **I am** going to meet you at the gate.

Some verbs, such as *be, have,* and *do,* have special forms in the singular and plural. Knowing these forms will help you in getting your subjects and verbs to agree.

Singular:	is, was	has	does
Plural:	are, were	have	do

A **Read each pair of sentences. Write A next to the sentence in which the subject and verb agree.**

1. _____ Lilly and Noah have decided to take their lambs to the fair.

    _____ Lilly and Noah has decided to take their lambs to the fair.

2. _____ Does Chris and Abby plan to stay overnight at the fairgrounds?

    _____ Do Chris and Abby plan to stay overnight at the fairgrounds?

3. _____ Neither my sisters nor my brother are interested in raising sheep.

    _____ Neither my sisters nor my brother is interested in raising sheep.

4. _____ Either one sheep or two small goats fit in this stall.

    _____ Either one sheep or two small goats fits in this stall.

5. _____ Zeb or Andrea grooms the lamb before the event.

    _____ Zeb or Andrea groom the lamb before the event.

6. _____ Seven white sheep and one black sheep are now entering the arena.

    _____ Seven white sheep and one black sheep is now entering the arena.

Advantage Grammar Grade 7 © 2005 Creative Teaching Press

B **Rewrite each sentence to correct subject-verb agreement.**

1. Games and rides is at the other end of the fairgrounds.

   _____

2. At one of the booths, my mother and sister is trying to win a goldfish.

   _____

3. Aiming and tossing the ball just right are difficult.

   _____

4. Neither I nor my friends was able to land a ball in one of the bowls.

   _____

5. My mother and sister enjoys games of all kinds.

   _____

C **Write a sentence in the present tense using the subject(s), conjunction, and a form of the verb provided. Reread your sentence to make sure the verb agrees with the subject.**

   Example: calf, goat / and / eat

   The calf and the goat are eating out of the same feeder.

1. Bacon, eggs / and / smell

   _____

2. Joseph, Jim, Amy / and / practice

   _____

3. Anne, Rasheed / or / plan

   _____

4. man, boys / and / stay

   _____

5. I, friends / neither . . . nor / know

   _____

Subject and Verb Agreement

★ Here are some other tips that will help you write sentences in which subjects and verbs agree:

• A prepositional phrase before the verb does not affect the verb.
> Only *one* of the judge's comments *was* negative.
> The *girls* by the barn *are* washing their goats.

• In sentences beginning with *there* or *here*, look for the subject after the verb.
> There *are* three *goats* by the barn.   Here *is* the *goat* that you lost.

• Collective nouns, which name a group of individuals, usually take a singular verb.
> The *crowd was* cheering loudly.

• Subjects that stand for amounts can be singular or plural. If the subject refers to a unit, the verb is singular. If it refers to several individual units, the verb is plural.
> *Ten miles is* too far to walk.
> *Half* of the people *are* standing.

• The title of a book, movie, or similar work of art is always treated as singular.
> *Roots was* a best-selling novel.

• Sometimes a subject is plural in form but singular in meaning.
> *Measles is* a common childhood disease.

A Underline the subject in each sentence. If the verb agrees with the subject, write *yes* on the line. If it does not agree, write *no*.

_____ **1.** Here are the winners in the showmanship competition.

_____ **2.** Sometimes members of the audience stands to applaud the winner.

_____ **3.** The exhibit on soil and water conservation lists tips for saving water.

_____ **4.** A schedule of daily events are posted at the entrance of each barn.

                                    Advantage Grammar Grade 7 © 2005 Creative Teaching Press

B Circle the form of the verb that correctly completes each sentence.

_____ **1.** There (is, are) three riding events that begin at nine o'clock.

_____ **2.** Some of the horses (wear, wears) ribbons in their manes and tails.

_____ **3.** *How to Rope Calves* (have helped, has helped) me prepare for the roping event.

_____ **4.** Two hours (are/is) is too long to wait in the check-in line.

_____ **5.** My family (is/are) rooting for me in the stands.

_____ **6.** Barrels (was, were) Aaron's favorite event at the horse show.

_____ **7.** (Does, do) five dollars cover what I owe you for lunch?

_____ **8.** One of the younger girls (ride, rides) a beautiful pinto pony.

_____ **9.** Strawberries and cream (was, were) a popular item on the menu.

_____ **10.** By the fence (are standing, is standing) my friends Ed and Leo in their cowboy hats.

C Use a present-tense verb and any other words to write a complete sentence.

1. The news about the winners _____

_____

2. Sheep and goats _____

_____

3. Half of the prize ribbon _____

_____

4. One of best parts _____

_____

5. Here is _____

_____

6. The audience _____

_____

Name _____

Fragments and Run-on Sentences

★ In most kinds of writing, you should avoid using sentence fragments and run-on sentences because they can be confusing to readers. A sentence fragment is a phrase or clause that expresses an incomplete thought. A fragment is often missing a subject or a verb. A sentence with a transitive verb but lacking a direct object is also a fragment.

Fragments: Because the canoe was leaking.
(Dependent clause standing alone)
That canoe, which is very lightweight.
(*Canoe* is the subject; its verb is missing.)
The man at the canoe rental gave us.
(*Gave* is transitive; the direct object is missing.)

Complete: We paddled fast because the canoe was leaking.
We tried that canoe, which is very lightweight.
The man at the canoe rental gave us two paddles.

A **run-on sentence** contains two or more main clauses that have been run together without proper punctuation or connecting words. To fix a run-on sentence, mark the end of each complete thought with a period, question mark, or exclamation mark. You may also need to reword or add transitions.

Run-on: Canoeing safety is important you should always wear a life vest.

Corrected: Canoeing safety is important. For example, you should always wear a life vest.

Ⓐ Read each sentence. On the line, write *F* if it is a sentence fragment. Write *C* if it is a complete sentence.

_____ **1.** We got up before sunrise and packed up the tent.

_____ **2.** Just a quick breakfast of hot tea and granola bars.

_____ **3.** We had tied the canoe to a log near the shore.

_____ **4.** Paddling across the calm lake.

_____ **5.** We paused to observe a heron along the shoreline.

Advantage Grammar Grade 7 © 2005 Creative Teaching Press

B **Rewrite each run-on sentence as two or more complete sentences.**

1. From the lake, we paddled to a stream the water was smooth at first.

   _____

   _____

2. Up ahead we could see swirls and bubbles and we could hear the water

   gurgling and we knew there were rocks under the water, although they didn't

   seem like big rocks. _____

   _____

   _____

3. Then we came to a stretch where the river was very shallow and our paddles

   dragged on the pebbles and then it got so shallow that we had to get out and

   pull the canoe that was hard work. _____

   _____

   _____

   _____

C **Write a paragraph describing a canoe trip on a lake or a river. Include sights, sounds, and things that happened. Then read your paragraph. Correct any sentence fragments or run-on sentences.**

   _____

   _____

   _____

   _____

   _____

   _____

   _____

Name _____

44

JUST FOR FUN

Capitalizing Proper Nouns and Adjectives

⭐ Proper nouns and proper adjectives are always capitalized. Here are some examples.

Months, days, holidays:	April, Tuesday, Memorial Day
Cites, town, states, countries:	Chicago, Brimfield, Kentucky, Mexico
Nationalities:	Brazilian, French, Japanese
Streets, bridges:	High Street, Brooklyn Bridge
Buildings, monuments:	John Hancock Building, Veterans Memorial
Bodies of water:	Lake Superior, Atlantic Ocean, Sugar Creek
Mountains and islands:	Mount Agassiz, Ellis Island
Other geographic features:	Lookout Trail, Hyde Park, Ohio River Valley
Organizations, businesses:	Ohio University, Parliament
Titles *before* proper names:	Mayor Smith, President Bill Clinton
Historical events, special events:	American Revolution, Rose Bowl
Religions and sacred writings:	Hinduism, the Bible

Ⓐ **Underline each word that should begin with a capital letter.**

1. Theodore roosevelt national park is named after our twenty-sixth president.

2. Roosevelt was born on october 27, 1858, in new york city.

3. He attended columbia law school briefly but soon entered politics.

4. He served in the legislature in new york for four years in the early 1880s.

5. In 1883 he went to the dakota territory to hunt buffalo and try his hand at cattle ranching.

6. He returned many times to this rugged land, where he gained a great respect for nature.

7. Back in politics two years later, Roosevelt held various political jobs including assistant secretary of the navy under president McKinley.

8. Roosevelt became a national hero during the spanish-american war when he led the charge up kettle hill in san juan, puerto rico.

9. After he became president, Roosevelt established five national parks and helped found the u.s. forest service.

10. The park that is named for Roosevelt is located in north dakota.

11. The visitors center is near medora, not far from the little missouri river.

12. Many take the scenic drive that goes to wind canyon and peaceful valley ranch.

Advantage Grammar Grade 7 © 2005 Creative Teaching Press

B Complete the phrase by writing an adjective from the box that is based on each proper noun.

Italian	Danish	Spanish	Democratic	Turkish	Elizabethan
Greek	Hawaiian	Islamic	Indian	Belgian	Vietnamese

1. India _____ curry

2. Spain _____ architecture

3. Denmark _____ furniture

4. Italy _____ soccer player

5. Hawaii _____ guitar

6. Turkey _____ rug

7. Belgium _____ chocolate

8. Queen Elizabeth _____ period

9. Vietnam _____ food

10. Islam _____ religion

11. Greece _____ temple

12. Democrat _____ party

C Give an example for each category from the town or region where you live.

1. street or road _____

2. monument _____

3. holiday _____

4. body of water _____

5. organization _____

6. business _____

7. special event _____

8. bridge _____

Name _____

★ Here are some more words that are often misspelled. Knowing how to spell these words can help you avoid many errors in your spelling.

magnificent	outrageous	responsibility	temperature
manageable	pastime	schedule	transparent
necessity	permanent	seize	twelfth
noticeable	persistent	separate	unnecessary
nutritious	procedure	significance	vehicle
occurrence	relieve	succeed	weird

A Write the word from the list above that fits each clue. The first letter is provided.

1. Not needed   u _ _ _ _ _ _ _ _ _ _

2. Not temporary   p _ _ _ _ _ _ _ _

3. After the eleventh   t _ _ _ _ _ _

4. A car or a truck   v _ _ _ _ _ _

5. Splendid   m _ _ _ _ _ _ _ _ _ _

6. Event   o _ _ _ _ _ _ _ _ _

B Complete each sentence with the correctly spelled word.

1. Charlie's favorite (pasttime, pastime) is attending science fiction conventions.

2. Picking up the tickets to the Latino Festival is Myra's (repsonsibility, responsibility).

3. Although it was a windy day, flying the kite was (manageable, managable).

4. Everyone wore (outrageous, outragious) costumes to the monster-theme party.

5. The Martian costume that Terri wore was especially (weird, weerd).

6. What is the (signifacence, significance) of those fluffy white clouds?

7. All of the food at the picnic was (nutritious, nutriceous) as well as yummy.

8. The (tempature, temperature) was over ninety, but we still played volleyball.

Name _____

C **Complete each sentence with a word from the list.**

> persistent   seize   noticeable   procedure
> succeed   necessity   transparent   schedule

1. A waterproof bag is a _____ when you go canoe camping.

2. If the bag is _____, you can easily see what is in it.

3. Did you _____ in reaching your goal of walking five miles a day?

4. You should _____ the opportunity if you are invited to go backpacking.

5. Danny was _____ in urging others to come along on the trip.

6. Marie's _____ allows her to walk the dog every afternoon.

7. Darla had a _____ sunburn on her arms after canoeing all day.

8. Kareem demonstrated the correct _____ for starting a campfire.

D **Find each of the listed words in the puzzle. Circle the entire word. The words may be read from top to bottom or from left to right.**

m	p	e	w	o	p	c	a	r	t
a	r	i	e	c	p	p	r	e	w
n	o	t	i	c	e	a	b	l	e
a	c	o	r	u	r	s	v	i	l
g	e	z	d	r	m	t	e	e	f
e	d	n	f	r	a	i	h	v	t
a	u	g	j	e	n	m	i	e	h
b	r	w	l	n	e	e	c	y	t
l	e	s	h	c	n	e	l	i	m
e	x	i	b	e	t	k	e	n	d

noticeable   occurrence
relieve   weird
vehicle   twelfth
permanent   pastime
procedure   manageable

Name _____

46

JUST FOR FUN

Rewriting Paragraphs for Correctness and Effectiveness

⭐ When you rewrite or revise a draft paragraph, you are looking for ways to improve its content and organization. This is also the time to correct any errors in spelling, grammar, punctuation, and word use. Here are some kinds of changes you may need to make as you rewrite a paragraph.

For Correctness	For Effectiveness
Complete sentences	Clearly stated main idea
Verb tense and agreement with subject	Appropriate supporting details
Agreement of pronouns and antecedents	Clear organization and appropriate transitions
Punctuation	Word choice
Spelling and word choice	Sentence variety
Use of negatives	Active voice

 Read and compare the draft paragraph and the rewritten paragraph below. Write the number of the sentence or sentences in the revision where each kind of improvement was made.

Draft

   There is a famous underwater creature. His name is the Loch Ness Monster. Or Nessie, as the monster is known. It has been reported by many peopol throughout history that they have spotted this monster in Loch Ness, a Scottish lake. They are about 30 feet long with a long neck, flipers, and a humped back.

Rewrite

   1) One of the most famous underwater creatures in the world is the Loch Ness Monster, or Nessie, as the monster is known. 2) Throughout history, many people have reported spotting this monster in a Scottish lake called Loch Ness. 3) People have described it as about 30 feet long, with a long neck, flippers, and a humped back.

1. Main idea is stated more clearly. _____

2. Misspelled word was corrected. _____

3. Passive voice was changed to active. _____

4. Antecedent of pronoun was clarified. _____

5. Sentence fragment was eliminated. _____

B Rewrite the paragraph below. Look for ways to improve the organization and correct any errors in grammar, punctuation, and spelling.

There isn't no actual proof that the Loch Ness Monsters exists. Some people will have taken photographs of something that seem to fit its description. To try to solve the mystery; scintists made several studies at Loch Ness using sonar equipment. The studies did not prove or disprove the existence of Nessie. This equipment can locate large objects under water by bouncing sound waves off it.

_____

_____

_____

_____

_____

_____

_____

_____

C Rewrite the paragraph below to make it more effective and correct.

Here's something interesting. A grainy black-and-white photograph shows the Loch Ness monster-or does it? The photograph was shot in 1934. Then it was sixty years later, the stepson of the photographer revealing that the photo was a fake. His stepfather has been making a model monster from a toy submarine and plastic wood that could be molded to holding a shape. The photograph was pased along to another person, who sold them to the newspaper.

_____

_____

_____

_____

_____

Name _____

LESSON

Editing Your Work

47

JUST FOR FUN

Editing your work is an important step in the writing process. Many tests ask you to show what you know about editing.

A **Read Raymond's article about the sport of orienteering. Then answer the questions that follow to help him revise and edit his article.**

Orienteering

1) Imagine a nature walk, a treasure hunt, and a track meet rolled into one. 2) That's the sport of orienteering. 3) It usually takes place in a park or forest. 4) The only tools you need is a compass and detailed map of the area.

5) At an orienteering event, or O-meet, each person gives a map of the area. 6) It is marked with a variety of courses. 7) Which vary in difficulty. 8) Your job is to follow the course by visiting a series of checkpoints shown on the map. 9) You are also given a list of clues to help you find the checkpoints. 10) A control card helps you keep track of your progress an official records your starting and ending time.

11) Using the map, you must decide on the best route to reach each checkpoint. 12) You might have to choose between a short route that takes you up and down a steep hill or a longer route on more level ground. 13) Because orienteering depends on map-reading ability and analyzing route choices, it is sometimes called "The Thinking Sport" or "Cunning Running."

1. In sentence 4, what change should be made so that the verb agrees with the compound subject? _____

2. In the second paragraph, which sentence should be changed to passive voice? Rewrite the sentence in the passive voice.

_____

3. Combine two sentences in the second paragraph to correct a sentence fragment.

_____

4. Which sentence in the second paragraph is a run-on sentence? _____

5. What transitional word or phrase should be added at the beginning of sentence 12? _____

Advantage Grammar Grade 7 © 2005 Creative Teaching Press

B **Raymond wrote an announcement for an orienteering event. Help him revise and edit his work by answering the questions below.**

Orienteering Meet
October 11–12
8:00 a.m. to 4:00 p.m.
Wolf Run regional park
1924 Yauger road
Mount Vernon, OH

1) Everyone is welcome to mount Vernon's first O-meet at our new regional park. 2) Participants of all ages and skill levels are welcome. 3) There is six separat courses, so you will be able to pick one that is manageble for you.

4) Each participant should bring their own compass. 5) Comfortable outdoor shoes are a must. 6) A long-sleeved shirt and long pants are also recommended for the required cross-country walking the terrain is hilly! 7) We are hoping for a magnifacent fall day, but this event will be held rain or shine.

8) Registration is at the park entrance. 9) Be sure to park your vehical in the marked area.

1. In the first six lines of the announcement, which words or phrases should be capitalized? _____

2. In sentence 1, which word should be capitalized? _____

3. What word should replace the word *is* in sentence 3?

_____

4. Rewrite sentence 4 to correct the mismatched pronoun and antecedent.

_____

_____

5. Sentences 3, 7, and 9 contain misspelled words. Write the words correctly.

_____

_____

6. How should the run-on sentence in the second paragraph be corrected?

_____

_____

Take a Test Drive

Fill in the bubble beside the correct answer.

Winnie wrote a report about Queen Elizabeth I of England. Read the first few paragraphs. Then, help her revise and edit her report by answering the questions below.

Good Queen Bess

1) Elizabeth I ruled England for forty-five years, from 1558 until she died in 1603. 2) During her reign, England became more united and more powerful as a nation, and both the arts and commerce thrived. 3) In fact, the Elizabethan era is regarded as one of the greatest periods in England's history.

4) Because Elizabeth was the daughter of King Henry VIII, it was expected that she might rule someday. 5) Since most rulers then were men, she would need to know and do the kinds of things that they did. 6) So she was educated like young men of the noble class. 7) With personal tutors, she studied history, geography, and mathematics. 8) And even astronomy and architecture. 9) She also learned how to speak French, Italian, Spanish, and Flemish, as well as the ancient languages of Greek and Latin.

10) Elizabeth was an eager and able student, and even as a young girl she had a strong will something that would help her when she became queen. 11) One of her favorite pasttimes were riding horseback, and she loved to ride fast. 12) She also loved to dance.

1. Which sentence is a run-on sentence?
- Ⓐ sentence 8
- Ⓒ sentence 10
- Ⓑ sentence 9
- Ⓓ none of the above

2. How could the third paragraph be improved?
- Ⓕ State the main idea more clearly.
- Ⓖ Make sure details relate to the main idea.
- Ⓗ Correct the subject-verb disagreement in sentence 11.
- Ⓙ All of the above.

3. Which of the following words in the third paragraph is misspelled?
- Ⓐ eager
- Ⓒ pasttimes
- Ⓑ something
- Ⓓ horseback

Advantage Grammar Grade 7 © 2005 Creative Teaching Press

Continue reading and editing Winnie's report. Answer the questions that follow.

1) The crowning of Elizabeth was a grand occasion. 2) As trumpets blared and drums played. 3) Elizabeth made her stately walk to the throne wearing beautiful gold robes. 4) Elizabeth wanted to look good, and she wanted her people to love her. 5) Many times during her reign she made great processions through the streets of London. 6) She wore dresses dripping with jewels as well as pearl necklaces and earrings. 7) People was excited to see the brilliant spectacle and especially to see the queen in person.

8) The people and parliament was expecting Elizabeth to marry, but she saw no necessity to get married. 9) She said that England was her husband. 10) Although she preferred to rule alone, she encouraged suitors. 11) Princes and dukes and the kings of other countries wanted to marry Elizabeth because they thought they could gain power over England by doing so. 12) Pretending to be interested helped Elizabeth achieve some of her political goals. 13) She knew her first responsbility was to bring peace and prosperity to her people.

4. Which sentence contains an error in capitalization?
- Ⓕ sentence 8
- Ⓖ sentence 9
- Ⓗ sentence 10
- Ⓙ sentence 11

5. Which is a sentence fragment that should be corrected?

Ⓐ sentence 1	Ⓒ sentence 3
Ⓑ sentence 2	Ⓓ sentence 4

6. Which would be the best word to replace *good* in sentence 4?

Ⓕ regal	Ⓗ young
Ⓖ well	Ⓙ mature

7. Which two sentences contain errors in subject-verb agreement?

Ⓐ 1 and 3	Ⓒ 10 and 11
Ⓑ 7 and 8	Ⓓ 12 and 13

8. In sentence 13, what is the correct spelling of the misspelled word?
- Ⓕ responsablity
- Ⓖ responsability
- Ⓗ responsibility
- Ⓙ responsebility

Practice Test

Read the paragraph and answer the questions.

1) Near the end of the Han dynasty [A.D. 220–264], the religion of Buddhism began to take hold in China. 2) Traders and missionaries from India have introduced the religion earlier, but it was not popular at first. 3) When barbarian invasions brought an end to the Han Empire, China fell into a state of disorder and uncertainty, and there was widespread suffering. 4) Because Buddhism offered the promise of an escape from suffering, it attracted many followers.

1. Which word in the paragraph should be capitalized?
   Ⓐ dynasty   Ⓒ but
   Ⓑ religion   Ⓓ state

2. What is the meaning of the prefixes *dis-* and *un-* in the words *disorder* and *uncertainty*?
   Ⓕ after   Ⓗ too much
   Ⓖ not   Ⓙ less than

3. What punctuation change should be made in sentence 1?
   Ⓐ Delete the comma.
   Ⓑ Move the comma inside the closing bracket.
   Ⓒ Change the brackets to parentheses.
   Ⓓ Change the period to an exclamation point.

4. Which change in sentence 2 is correct?
   Ⓕ Change *have* to *had*.
   Ⓖ Change *have* to *has*.
   Ⓗ Change *but* to *and*.
   Ⓙ Change *but* to *so*.

5. What type of sentence is sentence 4?
   Ⓐ Simple   Ⓒ Complex
   Ⓑ Compound   Ⓓ Fragment

6. What type of organization did the writer use in this paragraph?
   Ⓕ Chronological
   Ⓖ Order of importance
   Ⓗ Compare and contrast
   Ⓙ Cause and effect

Advantage Grammar Grade 4 © 2005 Creative Teaching Press

1) Buddhism is based on the teachings of Siddhartha Gautama, who was known as the Buddha. 2) His name means "Enlightened One." 3) The Buddha taught that suffering is part of life, however, though meditation a person could escape from suffering. 4) In his teachings the Buddha said, "Our life is shaped by our mind we become what we think". 5) According to the Buddha, suffering is caused by too much longing for the things we does not have.

7. What word(s) does the adjective clause in sentence 1 modify?
- Ⓐ Buddhism
- Ⓒ teachings
- Ⓑ is
- Ⓓ Siddhartha Gautama

8. Which sentence does NOT contain a clause in the passive voice?
- Ⓕ sentence 1
- Ⓗ sentence 4
- Ⓖ sentence 2
- Ⓙ sentence 5

9. What change should be made in sentence 3?
- Ⓐ Change the comma after *life* to a period.
- Ⓑ Change the comma after *life* to a semicolon.
- Ⓒ Change the comma after *however* to a semicolon.
- Ⓓ Delete the comma after *however*.

10. In sentence 4, what part of speech is *teachings*?
- Ⓕ verb
- Ⓗ gerund
- Ⓖ participle
- Ⓙ infinitive

11. Which statement about sentence 4 is true?
- Ⓐ It shows poor word choice.
- Ⓑ It has a punctuation errors.
- Ⓒ It contains a dangling modifier.
- Ⓓ It uses a double negative.

12. What error did the writer make in sentence 5?
- Ⓕ The subject and verb do not agree in number.
- Ⓖ The verb tense is not appropriate.
- Ⓗ The sentence contains a misplaced modifier.
- Ⓙ The adverb *too* is misspelled.

Practice Test

Read this description of a national park. Then answer the questions that follow.

1) Everything in Sequoia and Kings Canyon National Park is big. Giant sequoias grow here. 2) The sequoia is taller than any other type of tree, and they has a huge trunk. 3) Perhaps you have seen old photographs of people driving wagons though a hole carved in the base of one of these trees. 4) This national park also contains the highest mountain in the lower forty eight states: Mount Whitney. 5) The park also has the deepest canyon in North America. 6) Kings Canyon, with its steep granite walls, plunges more than 8,000 feet from its rim to the Kings River below not even the Grand Canyon is as deep as this canyon.

13. What kind of supporting details did the writer use in the paragraph?
- Ⓐ facts
- Ⓑ examples
- Ⓒ reasons
- Ⓓ statistics

14. How many prepositions are there in sentence 3?
- Ⓕ one
- Ⓖ two
- Ⓗ three
- Ⓙ four

15. Which two words should be joined by a hyphen to form one word?
- Ⓐ people-driving
- Ⓑ forty-eight
- Ⓒ North-America
- Ⓓ 8,000-feet

16. In sentence 2, what word should replace the word *they*?
- Ⓕ he
- Ⓖ she
- Ⓗ it
- Ⓙ I

17. Which words in the paragraph have suffixes that show comparison?
- Ⓐ photographs and trees
- Ⓑ carved and plunges
- Ⓒ steep and even
- Ⓓ taller and deepest

18. How should the run-on problem in sentence 6 be fixed?
- Ⓕ Change the comma after *canyon* to a period, and capitalize *with*.
- Ⓖ Change the comma after *walls* to a period, and capitalize *plunges*.
- Ⓗ Add a period after *feet*, and capitalize *from*.
- Ⓙ Add a period after *below*, and capitalize *not*.

   Advantage Grammar Grade 4 © 2005 Creative Teaching Press

Answer Key

Lesson 1
A
1. Genghis Khan, ruler, Mongols, 1200s
2. Mongols, Asia, plains, steppes
3. They (pronoun), clans, kinship
4. clans, tribe
5. chief, tribe, courage, ability, leadership
6. chief, men, tribes loyalty, him (pronoun)
7. Mongols, skill, horseback
8. they (pronoun), horse, their (pronoun), feet, they (pronoun), their (pronoun), weapons, they (pronoun)
9. skill, soldiers, advantage, battle
10. Khan, his (pronoun), warriors, amount, land, Beijing, Caspian Sea

B
1. person
2. thing
3. idea
4. place, proper
5. thing
6. thing
7. idea
8. person, proper
9. place, proper
10. persons, proper

C
Answers will vary in some cases. Possible answers:
1. George Washington, he
2. city, it
3. teacher, Ms. Wu
4. country, it
5. invaders, they
6. Shania Twain, she
7. monument, Lincoln Memorial
8. people, the Harrisons

D
Answers will vary.

Lesson 2
A
1. study, feel
2. refers, began, write
3. is, remain
4. include
5. developed
6. exist, study
7. are
8. produced

B
1. b
2. a
3. b
4. b
5. a
6. a
7. b
8. a

C
Answers will vary. Possible answers:
1. I <u>took</u> the bus to school.
2. I <u>learned</u> about samurai warriors in Japan.
3. I <u>have been thinking</u> about my kung fu class.
4. I <u>will be</u> at school tomorrow.

Lesson 3
A
1. can
2. anybody
3. anybody
4. a
5. anything
6. ever

B
Answers may vary, but each corrected sentence should include only one negative word.
1. Correct
2. Sam has no energy to attend his kung fu class.
3. Is nobody going to give a report on the samurai?
4. It won't make any difference if they are five minutes late.
5. We won't have any time to visit the Zen garden at the museum.
6. I've never seen a Japanese tea ceremony before.
7. No one in the class had ever heard of Kublai Khan before.
8. Correct

C
Answers will vary but should include four of the listed phrases.

Lesson 4
A
1. As an island, Japan was isolated from the world; thus, it developed with little influence from other countries except China.
2. Japan is located on a very unstable part of the earth's crust; therefore earthquakes are common there.
3. Typhoons are also frequent in Japan; these are coastal storms with tree-bending winds and heavy rains.
4. For thousands of years, the sea has been Japan's greatest resource; it has provided food and shielded the island from invasion.
5. A Japanese myth describes how the world began; two sky gods decided to create the islands of Japan by dipping a jeweled spear into the ocean.
6. Some of the earliest inhabitants of Japan were the Jomon; they probably came from Korea.
7. Early peoples believed in the power of natural spirits; these spirits were called kami.
8. The Sun Goddess was the most powerful of the kami; Japan's first emperor claimed to be descended from the Sun Goddess.

B
1. Hunter-gatherers lived in Japan in prehistoric times, and the Ainu people of northern Japan may be related to them.
2. The Jomon developed a complex culture; they used irrigation to create wet fields where they cultivated rice.
3. The next civilization, the Yayoi, was called the "tomb culture," for the Yayoi built huge graves.
4. The graves contained small clay figures of soldiers and horses; these objects suggest that the Yayoi took part in wars and respected warriors.
5. Japan is an island, but one of its main religions, Buddhism, comes from China.

Answer Key

6. Japan's ruler in the 600s, Prince Shotoku, welcomed Buddhist priests; they helped introduce the Chinese language and arts in Japan.
7. After Shotoku's death, government leaders introduced Chinese-style reforms; all land was made the property of the emperor.
8. These reforms reduced the power of the clan leaders; however, the lives of everyday peasants did not change much.

C
Paragraphs should include at least two compound sentences. Students should use semicolons or commas correctly in these sentences.

Lesson 5
A
1. cheaper, cheapest
2. tougher, toughest
3. sturdier, sturdiest
4. darker, darkest
5. friendlier, friendliest
6. sooner, soonest
7. deadlier, deadliest
8. freer, freest
9. narrower, narrowest
10. tastier, tastiest
11. later, latest
12. heartier, heartiest

B
1. safer
2. bravest
3. earlier
4. soonest
5. bluest
6. angrier
7. longer
8. worthiest
9. fewer
10. plainest
11. costliest
12. nearest
13. sadder
14. older

Lesson 6
A
Answers may vary but should be similar to the following.

In first draft	In revision	more colorful	more precise	more appropriate
1. really cool	beautiful	x	x	x
2. Japanese religion	Buddhism		x	
3. do	create		x	
4. little	tiny		x	
5. scene	natural scene	x	x	
6. a groovy way	neat patterns		x	x
7. special	quiet and peaceful		x	
8. thinking	meditation		x	

B
Word choices will vary. Sample revision.
The samurai of Japan were the *warriors* of medieval Japan. They were similar to knights in medieval Europe. They both *rode* horses and *wore* armor. The samurai's armor was made up of many small plates of steel *sewn* together with leather strips. Knights, on the other hand, wore armor made of large curved *plates* of steel. Both samurai and knights swore loyalty to a lord and started their training while they were *young*. Both were *members* of a warrior class that had a special code of *conduct*.

C
Words chosen and replacements will vary. Some possible responses are listed.

In first draft	In revision	more colorful	more precise	more appropriate
fighters	warriors	x	x	
had	rode		x	
had	wore		x	
brought	sewn		x	
hunks	plates	x	x	x
little	young		x	
parts	members		x	
doing	conduct		x	x

Lesson 7
A
1. Great Wall; because it is a proper noun
2. This long wall runs from east to west along the northern *border* (or *boundary*) of China.
3. runs; intransitive; because there is no object after the verb
4. Replace the comma after *high* with a semicolon.
5. *Emperor* is more specific and colorful.
6. The Great Wall today is about 4,000 miles long; however, that includes many branches.

B
1. Most of them were ordered to do the work; they did not volunteer.
2. enemies
3. wall
4. because the clauses are joined by the conjunction *and*
5. state-of-being verbs
6. Many workers must have thought, "This wall will never be finished."
7. sturdier

Lesson 8
A
1. B
2. H
3. C
4. F
5. C
6. G
7. A
8. H

Lesson 9
A
1. constant→companion
2. complete→journey
3. bright→moon
4. whole→side, full→moon
5. powerful→light
6. changing→shape
7. different→shapes
8. large→shadow, crescent→moon

B
1. very→beautiful (adj)
2. conveniently→was rising (v)
3. extremely→hard (adv), hard→had been working (v)
4. happily→continued (v)
5. Even→today (adv), today→call (v)

C

Adjectives: smiley, high, modern, original, serious, few, every, energetic, late, southern, cool, tasty
Adverbs: very, not, high, quickly, rarely, extremely, quite, late, truly, almost

Lesson 10

A

1. C		5. C	
2. P		6. C	
3. P		7. C	
4. P		8. P	

B

Answers will vary.

C

1. Comets are made of ice, stones, dust, and lumps of metal.
2. Asteroids are small objects made of rock, but "small" can mean 600 miles across.
3. We had forgotten our special sunglasses, so we did not look directly at the solar eclipse.
4. I will do a science project on comets and asteroids.

Lesson 11

A

1. Although tired; dangling
2. To be considered among the top science students; dangling
3. in a black frame; misplaced.

B

Answers will vary but may be similar to the following.
1. Before going home, we saw that a full moon had risen over the treetops.
2. The speaker ignored the students, although they were noisy and excited.
3. Staying out to look at the winter sky, I nearly froze my ears.
4. As we looked out the car window, we could see the lunar eclipse beginning.
5. A guide met the students as they stepped inside the air and space museum.

C

Answers may vary but should be similar to the following.
1. We bought only a few souvenirs when we went to the space center.
2. With a sigh, Arnie picked up the guide to stars that his father had given him.
3. After much deliberation, the science editor he had written to rejected his article.
4. We went almost to the end of the dirt road before we set up the telescope.
5. With our binoculars, several of us spotted the Sea of Tranquility on the moon.

Lesson 12

A

1. C		5. C	
2. I		6. C	
3. I		7. I	
4. I		8. C	

B

1. Seestars writes, "They [the streaks] may look like falling stars, but they are really the trails of meteors."
2. Bits of rock (and also metal) exist in the space between Earth and the other planets.
3. Bits that are closer to Earth fall toward it (and us) because of gravity.
4. The particles fall very fast (at up to 150,000 miles [250,000 km] per hour).
5. Friction (rubbing) with the air in Earth's atmosphere heats them up.
6. The rock bits burn up and leave a fiery trail (what we see as a meteor).

C

1. (August 12, 2005).
2. (we went to the Rockies)
3. (elevation 14,110 feet [4,301 meters])
4. (he teaches at the local college)

Lesson 13

A

1. relays		6. tries	
2. pushes		7. greets	
3. taxes		8. sizzles	
4. relates		9. surrounds	
5. refers		10. denies	

B

1. viewed		5. delayed	
2. tried		6. referred	
3. renewing		7. sitting	
4. jogging			

Lesson 14

A

1. The largest one, which is 567 miles in diameter, is called Ceres. *Replaces*: One of them is called Ceres. It is the largest. Its diameter is 567 miles.
2. While Ceres is as big as a small moon, most asteroids are smaller than 10 miles in diameter. *Replaces*: Ceres is as big as a small moon. Most asteroids are smaller than 10 miles in diameter.

B

Paragraphs will vary. A sample paragraph is given.
The spacecraft *Galileo* visited two asteroids when it was on its way to Jupiter. Asteroids, unlike planets and moons, can be lumpy. One of the asteroids near Jupiter, named Gaspra, is shaped like a potato. It also has a few craters, which were made by meteorites. The other asteroid, named Ida, has its own little moon.

Answer Key

Lesson 15

A
1. adjectives; both modify the noun *ways*
2. sentence 2; travels; traveled
3. Sentence 8: To see how, try this experiment (from the book *Earth and Sun* [1998]). Sentence 10: Insert the pencil through the center of the ball (to represent Earth and its axis).

B
1. After dimming the room lights, turn on the flashlight and point it at the ball. (The missing subject, *you*, is implied in a command.)
2. Notice that the sun *shines* directly on the southern (bottom) hemisphere.
3. after *top*
4. This situation represents summer in the Southern Hemisphere and winter in the Northern Hemisphere.
5. preposition; it has an object and it tells something about another part of the sentence (where the North Pole is).

Lesson 16

A
1. B
2. G
3. B
4. H
5. D
6. H
7. D
8. G

Lesson 17

A
1. I
2. D
3. C
4. E
5. D
6. C
7. D
8. E
9. D
10. I

B
1. Park.
2. Everglades?
3. boat.
4. grass.
5. islands.
6. water.
7. panther.
8. Wow! . . . fish!
9. Trail?
10. ecosystem.

C
Answers will vary. Sample sentences are given.
1. Did you see any ospreys or pelicans? (int)
   Look at that huge osprey! (exc)
   Notice the osprey's large wingspan. (imp)
2. The alligator has many sharp teeth. (dec)
   Did you see the alligator open its mouth? (int)
   Don't approach that alligator. (imp)
3. Come on! (exc)
   The walk to Nine Mile Pond is only half a mile. (dec)
   Will you walk with me to Nine Mile Pond? (int)

Lesson 18

A
1. completed
2. continuing
3. continuing

B
1. will have set
2. had soaked
3. had been smoking
4. had turned
5. had been hiking

C
1. had left
2. have been listening
3. had stayed
4. will have covered
5. had heard
6. had been living
7. has been coming
8. had owned

Lesson 19

A
1. that we saw➡formations
2. which is in southern Utah➡park
3. who take the scenic drive to Devil's Garden➡people
4. who is leading the hike through Fiery Furnace➡ranger
5. whom we met on the trail➡Ranger Dogood
6. who enjoy the stunning scenery➡visitors
7. which looks indestructible➡land

B
1. The park, which was established in 1971, has more than 2,000 natural arches.
2. Essential
3. Essential
4. Forces in the earth's crust, which became unstable, tilted and lifted up the beds of sand.
5. Frost, snow, and rain eroded the soft rock, which has taken on fantastic shapes as a result.
6. The formations, whose colors include pink, lavender, and orange, are still eroding.
7. Coyotes, bobcats, and foxes, which come out at night, are native to the area.
8. Essential

C
Answers may vary depending on which clause is subordinated. Possible answers:
1. The hike, which is led by a naturalist, starts at sunrise.
2. The author Edward Abbey, who lived in the park, wrote a book called *Desert Solitaire*.
3. The rock formation that Jane likes best is Skyline Arch.

Lesson 20

A
1. This road takes you past several geysers: Grand Geyser, Lone Star Geyser, and Old Faithful.
2. At precisely 7:52 a.m., Old Faithful sent a great plume of water one hundred feet into the air.

Advantage Grammar Grade 7 © 2005 Creative Teaching Press

3. Along the roadside, Belinda saw many signs with these words: Deer Crossing.
4. There were five young people on the bicycle tour: Donny, Martin, Liz, Kiesha, and Tom.
5. Remember: Always stay on the marked trails.
6. The ranger had this comment as we approached Old Faithful: "Enjoy the show from the safety of the boardwalk."
7. My uncle, a photographer, gave me some good advice: When taking pictures of geysers, always use a fast shutter speed.
8. During our stay in Yellowstone, we saw the following animals: bison, bighorn sheep, beavers, mink, and moose.
9. Jan read aloud from the booklet *Observing Wildlife: Do's and Don'ts.*
10. The park offers many conveniences: post offices, photo shops, boat rentals, and bus tours.

B
Colons should be added as follows:
Dear Ms. Jimenez:
8:00 to 12:00 a.m. or 12:00 to 4:00 p.m.
have agreed to pick up litter:

C
Answers will vary but should include a colon after the greeting and one in an expression of time.

Lesson 21
A

1. irregular	5. reenter
2. illegible	6. overrun
3. unnoticed	7. unneeded
4. dissatisfied	8. misstated

B
1. impatient—not patient
2. irresponsible—not responsible
3. prepay—pay before
4. nonsense—something with no meaning
5. miscalculate—calculate incorrectly
6. overreact—react too much
7. uncertain—not certain
8. rearrange—arrange again
9. overeat—eat too much
10. impossible—not possible
11. reassemble—assemble again
12. subtitle—title below
13. uncomfortable—not comfortable
14. posttest—a test afterward
15. inaccurate—not accurate
16. depress—press down

C
Answers will vary.

Lesson 22
A
(topic sentence) We need to do everything we can to save the Everglades.
A. The Everglades is a diverse ecosystem.
1. It has hundreds of types of plants and over 300 kinds of birds.
2. It has mammals such as the manatee and Florida panther.
B. This fragile ecosystem is threatened.
1. There are far fewer ibises than before.
2. The manatee, crocodile, and Florida panther are endangered.

B
Paragraphs will vary in wording but may be similar to the following. All listed facts should be included.
Kilauea, which lies partly within Hawaii Volcanoes National Park, is a young volcano that is still active. The volcano, whose name means "much spewing," has erupted more than fifty times since 1980. In the 1980s, a number of violent eruptions caused much damage along the park's eastern border. In the 1989 eruption, molten rock from the volcano swept away one of the visitors centers in the park. After these repeated eruptions, the cone of the volcano had risen to over 700 feet tall.

Lesson 23
A
1. Supporting details are facts.
2. that are open to the public; yes
3. We got to the visitors center at 8:00 a.m.
4. They are all declarative.
5. We were glad we brought our jackets.

B
1. Change the semicolon after the word *from* to a colon.
2. which is two hours long
3. preview; before
4. As I walked along, one question stayed in my *mind*: How dark would it be without any light at *all*?
5. Change the period to an exclamation point, because the sentence expresses strong feeling.
6. By the time we got back to daylight, the sky *had clouded* over, but it was still hard to adjust to the brightness.

Lesson 24

1. D	5. A
2. G	6. J
3. B	7. C
4. J	8. F

Lesson 25
A
1. to do
2. to chew your food
3. to swallow
4. to digest starches in the food
5. No infinitive
6. to move into the esophagus

Answer Key

7. No infinitive
8. to fill up with food
9. to break down proteins in the food
10. to mix the food with its highly acidic juices

B
Answers will vary. Possible answers:
1. to eat a lot of junk food.
2. To cook spaghetti
3. to explain the digestive system.
4. to read the recommendations in the food pyramid.
5. to find out about the nutrients in foods.
6. to lose some weight.
7. to have a balanced diet
8. to chew your food thoroughly.
9. to serve apple pie with ice cream.
10. to consume more fruits and vegetables.

C
Responses will vary.

Lesson 26
A
1, 3, 4, and 7 are past participles; 2, 5, and 6 are present participles. Sentences will vary.

B
1. food
2. tube
3. path, path
4. chemicals
5. nubs

C
1. *called* villi
2. *absorbed* into the bloodstream
3. *Traveling* in the blood
4. *storing* others until needed

D
1. All food comes from *living* things.
2. A *varied* diet will help you to stay healthy.
3. A *balanced* diet contains the right amounts of proteins, carbohydrates, fats, minerals, and vitamins.

Lesson 27
A
1. A
2. A
3. A
4. A
5. P
6. P
7. A
8. A
9. A
10. P

B
1. I ate my food too quickly, so I got the hiccups.
2. Sometimes you can cure the hiccups by holding your breath.
3. The fastest sprinter won the race.
4. With each breath, you inhale and exhale about two cupfuls of air.
5. When you sneeze, air is expelled from your nose at 99 miles per hour!

C Possible answer:
1. The singer took a deep breath. With this air she could sing a long musical phrase. The sound of her voice filled the concert hall. The audience applauded the singer enthusiastically.

Lesson 28
A
1. warm-up
2. hard-playing
3. soft-spoken
4. self-confidence
5. ex-president
6. hair-raising

B
1. On Saturday—or perhaps it was Sunday—we went to the track meet.
2. If you see Dwayne—wait a minute, there he is now—tell him we'll be at the gate.
3. It was an amazing race—a race that I will never forget.
4. Jerry—I don't know if he can win or not—just completed the first lap of the race.
5. His finishing time—this is incredible—was three minutes and fifteen seconds!

C
1. knife-edged sword
2. high-flying kite
3. one-sided story
4. well-to-do family

D
1. b
2. c
3. a
4. d

Lesson 29
A
1. playfully
2. coolly
3. typically
4. terribly
5. ably
6. openly
7. efficiently
8. bodily
9. carefully
10. strongly
11. rapidly
12. dully
13. forcefully
14. completely
15. doubly
16. busily

B
1. thinness
2. painfulness
3. suddenness
4. happiness
5. openness
6. heaviness
7. shortness
8. largeness

C
1. medically
2. sweaty
3. totally
4. fully
5. icy
6. possibly
7. trickiness
8. agreeably

Lesson 30
A
1. two main jobs; First; Second
2. As a result; so

3. on the other hand

B
1. The most important
2. Also,
3. For example,
4. In fact,

C
1. C, First, Then, Finally
2. CE, Therefore, Another result
3. S, Below, left, right; or Below, right, left

Lesson 31
A
1. to emphasize the phrase that follows
2. sentence 2
3. to give a pint of blood
4. People can donate blood at a clinic or any bloodmobile.
5. Recently, I visited a bloodmobile with my dad, who had decided to give blood.
6. self-sacrifice

B
1. yes; full + ly
2. participle (present); bag
3. two-thirds; light-headed
4. to contrast the points made in sentences 7 and 8
5. past; as an adjective
6. To give blood

Lesson 32
1. B   5. B
2. F   6. F
3. B   7. D
4. J   8. G

Lesson 33
A
1. gathering ideas and information
2. finding information
3. Locating books at the library
4. classifying books
5. No gerund
6. Becoming familiar with the Dewey Decimal System
7. finding out the call number
8. typing in a search in the online catalog
9. writing down the call number
10. using the signs at the ends of the bookshelves
11. book signing
12. diving

B
1. Missing the bus made him late for school.
2. You should give swimming a try.
3. Containing our excitement was impossible.
4. Will you help me with collecting the books?
5. My aunt is fond of treating us to ice cream.
6. Try searching for that book with a keyword.

C
1. consulting   4. catching
2. looking   5. Using

3. browsing   6. Improving

Lesson 34
A
1. Lawrence
2. poem
3. Eve Merriam and Nikki Giovanni
4. Eve Merriam
5. audience
6. three students

B
1. All of the students said they would help.
2. Nobody remembered to bring his or her notebook.
3. Many in the audience said that poetry gives them comfort.
4. Every one of the girls was giving the speaker her complete attention.
5. Everybody liked the poem, but three or four said they loved it.

C
1. Someone left *his* (or *her*) notebook on one of the seats at the poetry reading.
2. Each of the poems has *its* own theme.
3. The three poets were at the bookstore. All had agreed to sign *their* books.
4. Cassandra gave *her* most expressive reading yet of Frost's poem "Birches."
5. Make sure that each reader has somebody to listen to *her* (or *him*).

Lesson 35
A
1. because they are about the natural world.
2. After I read "Mute Dancers: How to Watch a Hummingbird,"
3. If you want to learn some fascinating facts about hummingbirds
4. as they speed or dart from flower to flower.
5. When a hummingbird drinks nectar
6. Because this tiny bird's heart beats 500 times a minute
7. When the day ends
8. At night while the hummingbird is resting

B
1. C   5. voices,
2. lands,   6. C
3. C   7. message,
4. C   8. shirt,

C
1. We were delighted when we saw six hummingbirds at the feeder at one time.
2. There are more kinds of hummingbirds near the equator because there are more flowers in warm climates.
3. We could see hummingbirds wherever we looked in Mrs. Holman's garden.
4. Although there are 16 species of hummingbirds in North America, there are dozens of species in South America.

Answer Key

Lesson 36
A
1. A Tibetan proverb states, "The goal will not be reached if the right distance is not traveled."
2. "In spite of everything," Anne Frank wrote in her diary, "I still believe that people are really good at heart."
3. "Reading is to the mind what exercise is to the body," wrote the eighteenth-century British author Richard Steele.

B
1. For the poetry reading, Stan is planning to read "How to Eat a Poem" by Eve Merriam.
2. After reading the newspaper, she clipped the article "How to Chop an Onion in Four Easy Steps."
3. Last weekend, we watched the movie Star Wars plus all of the sequels.
4. "By the Light of the Silvery Moon" is a very old-fashioned song that is often played on ukulele.
5. At the library, I chose The Moon by Whale Light, a nonfiction book by Diane Ackerman.
6. "The Last Leaf" is a typical O. Henry short story because it has a surprise ending.
7. "I'll Fly Away" is a folk song about escaping from prison, slavery, or some other unhappy situation.
8. Zeb likes to read the sports pages in USA Today, a very popular newspaper.
9. The Diary of Anne Frank was first performed at the Cort Theater in New York City in 1955.
10. "The Tell-Tale Heart" is one of Edgar Allan Poe's most famous and most chilling short stories.

C
Answers will vary, but each sentence should identify the speaker of the quoted words.

Lesson 37
A
1. absence
2. conscious
3. eighth
4. answer
5. column
6. independent

B
1. leisure
2. breathe
3. acquaintance
4. accessible
5. efficiency
6. attendance

C
1. finally
2. lightning
3. influential
4. existence
5. committee
6. clothes
7. business
8. accurate

D

Lesson 38
A
1. your tired, your poor, your huddled masses
2. of the people, by the people, for the people
3. it was the best of times; it was the worst of times
4. everyone is equal; everyone is free
5. champions aren't made in gyms; champions are made from something they have inside them—a desire, a dream, a vision

B
1. He described the rose as soft, delicate, and sweet-smelling.
2. In his letter, he says he likes swimming, waterskiing, and playing chess.
3. World War II was fought on the land, on the sea, and in the air.
4. My goals are to do my best, to treat others kindly, and to have a good time.
5. It's a bird! It's a plane! No, it's Superman!

C
Paragraphs will vary but should include at least two examples of parallel form.

Lesson 39
A
1. In the essay "Paul Bunyan of the North Woods," Carl Sandburg retells some of the popular stories about Paul Bunyan.
2. influential
3. He is a giant of a man and a very strong man.
4. before "Some" and after alphabet, following the period
5. sentence 9
6. as different writers wrote down the tales

B
1. abundant
2. men; his disagrees with men in number. To grease the griddle for pancakes, four men strapped big pieces of pork to their snowshoes and skated across the griddle.
3. eating
4. They are similar in grammatical form and wording. The similarity helps the reader follow the writer's thoughts.

Advantage Grammar Grade 7 © 2005 Creative Teaching Press

5. sentence 7

Lesson 40
A
1. C
2. F
3. D
4. H
5. B
6. G
7. D
8. J

Lesson 41
A
1. Lilly and Noah have decided to take their lambs to the fair.
2. Do Chris and Abby plan to stay overnight at the fairgrounds?
3. Neither my sisters nor my brother is interested in raising sheep.
4. Either one sheep or two small goats fit in this stall.
5. Zeb or Andrea grooms the lamb before the event.
6. Seven white sheep and one black sheep are now entering the arena.

B
1. Games and rides are at the other end of the fairgrounds.
2. At one of the booths, my mother and sister *are* trying to win a goldfish.
3. Aiming and tossing the ball just right *is* difficult.
4. Neither I nor my friends *were* able to do it.
5. My mother and sister *enjoy* games of all kinds.

C
1. Bacon and eggs smells good first thing in the morning.
2. Joseph, Jim, and Amy are practicing for the talent show.
3. Anne or Rasheed plans to visit the art museum.
4. That man and those boys are staying late to finish the painting.
5. Neither I nor my friends know a shortcut to the school.

Lesson 42
A
1. winners; yes
2. members; no
3. exhibit; yes
4. schedule; no

B
1. are
2. wear
3. has helped
4. is
5. is
6. was
7. Does
8. rides
9. was
10. are standing

C
Answers will vary but should show subject-verb agreement.

Lesson 43
A
1. C
2. F
3. C
4. F

5. C

B
Answers may vary but should be similar to the following:
1. From the lake we paddled to a stream. The water was smooth at first.
2. Up ahead we could see swirls and bubbles, and we could hear the water gurgling. We knew there were rocks under the water, although they didn't seem like big rocks.
3. Then we came to a stretch where the river was very shallow, and our paddles dragged on the pebbles. Then it got so shallow that we had to get out and pull the canoe! That was hard work.

C
Paragraphs will vary but should include only complete sentences.

Lesson 44
A
1. Theodore Roosevelt National Park is named after our twenty-sixth president.
2. Roosevelt was born on October 27, 1858, in New York City.
3. He attended Columbia Law School briefly but soon entered politics.
4. He served in the state assembly in New York for four years in the early 1880s.
5. In 1883 he went to the Dakota Territory to hunt buffalo and try his hand at cattle ranching.
6. no capital letters needed
7. Back in politics two years later, Roosevelt held various political jobs including assistant secretary of the navy under President McKinley.
8. Roosevelt became a national hero during the Spanish-American War after he led the charge up Kettle Hill in San Juan, Puerto Rico.
9. After he became president, Roosevelt established five national parks and helped found the U.S. Forest Service.
10. The park that is named for Roosevelt is located in North Dakota.
11. The visitors center is near Medora, not far from the Little Missouri River.
12. Many take the scenic drive that goes to Wind Canyon and Peaceful Valley Ranch.

B
1. Indian
2. Spanish
3. Danish
4. Italian
5. Hawaiian
6. Turkish
7. Belgian
8. Elizabethan
9. Vietnamese
10. Islamic
11. Greek
12. Democratic

C
Answers will vary.

Answer Key

Lesson 45

A
1. unnecessary
2. permanent
3. twelfth
4. vehicle
5. magnificent
6. occurrence

B
1. pastime
2. responsibility
3. manageable
4. outrageous
5. weird
6. significance
7. nutritious
8. temperature

C
1. necessity
2. transparent
3. succeed
4. seize
5. persistent
6. schedule
7. noticeable
8. procedure

D

Lesson 46

A
1. 1
2. 2, 3
3. 2
4. 3
5. 1

B
Rewrites may be reworded as follows. All errors in grammar, usage, and mechanics should be corrected.

There is no actual proof that the Loch Ness Monster exists. However, some people have taken photographs of something that seems to fit its description. To try to solve the mystery, scientists made several studies at Loch Ness using sonar equipment. This equipment can locate large objects under water by bouncing sound waves off them. The studies did not prove or disprove the existence of Nessie. (Last two sentences have been transposed.)

C
Rewrites should be similar to the following.

A grainy black-and-white photograph shows the Loch Ness Monster—or does it? The photograph was shot in 1934. Sixty years later, the stepson of the photographer revealed that the photo was a fake. His stepfather had made a model monster from a toy submarine and plastic wood that could be molded to hold a shape. The

photograph was passed along to another person, who sold it to the newspaper.

Lesson 47

A
1. Change *is* to *are*.
2. sentence 5: At an orienteering event, or O-meet, each person is given a map of the area.
3. It is marked with a variety of courses, which vary in difficulty.
4. sentence 10
5. For example,

B
1. Regional Park, Road
2. Mount
3. are
4. Each participant should bring *his* or *her* own compass.
5. separate, manageable, magnificent, vehicle
6. Add a period after *walking,* and capitalize the word *the.*

Lesson 48
1. C
2. J
3. C
4. F
5. B
6. F
7. B
8. H

Practice Test
1. A
2. G
3. C
4. F
5. C
6. J
7. D
8. G
9. B
10. H
11. B
12. F
13. B
14. J
15. B
16. H
17. D
18. J

Advantage Grammar Grade 7 © 2005 Creative Teaching Press